The

e-commerce

Question and Answer Book

The

e-commerce
Question and Answer Book

A SURVIVAL GUIDE FOR BUSINESS MANAGERS

Anita Rosen

AMACOM
American Management Association
New York • Atlanta • Boston • Chicago • Kansas City • San Francisco • Washington, D. C.
Brussels • Mexico City • Tokyo • Toronto

This publication is designed to provide accurate and authoritative information in regard to the subject matter covered. It is sold with the understanding that the publisher is not engaged in rendering legal, accounting, or other professional service. If legal advice or other expert assistance is required, the services of a competent professional person should be sought.

Microsoft and Windows are trademarks or registered trademarks of Microsoft Corporation. Netscape and Netscape Navigator are trademarks or registered trademarks of Netscape Communications Corporation. Barbie is a registered trademark of Mattel, Inc.

Library of Congress Cataloging-in-Publication Data

Rosen, Anita.
     The E-commerce question and answer book / Anita Rosen.
          p.   cm.
     Includes index.
     ISBN 0-8144-0525-8
     1. Electronic commerce.   I. Title.
HF5548.32.R67m1999
658.8'00285'46 21—dc21   99-040100

Printing number

10   9   8   7   6   5   4   3   2   1

This book is dedicated to my mother, Arlette Rosen.

*Special thanks to Al Moser, Anita and Andy Moser,
Chapman Greer, and Jacquie Flynn for all their support and help
with the creation of this book*

Contents

Chapter 3: E-Commerce Technology   66

Introduction

The explosion of the Internet, and most recently e-commerce, has posed a particularly interesting dilemma for most businesses. The dilemma is:

- How should we integrate e-commerce with our business?
- Where do we start?
- What resources do we need?
- What skills do we need?
- How do we make e-commerce a success for our company?

The goal of this book is to provide businesspeople with a comprehensive understanding of e-commerce and to answer their e-commerce questions. This book starts by explaining market considerations. In chapter two, the book provides the reader with the skills to understand how he can integrate e-commerce into his business. In chapter three, we discuss the technologies of e-commerce on the Internet. In chapter four, we join business direction and technologies to help the reader obtain an implementation strategy. This book provides the reader with the latest information on successfully marketing his site.

Readers might like to skim chapters for a basic understanding and then concentrate on a subject that is of particular interest. This book is organized for this method of learning. Each chapter is broken into sections. Each section starts with an overview consisting of a statement and bullet points. After the section overview, there is a section on the subject labeled "Tell Me More." "Tell Me More" provides the reader with a comprehensive understanding of the topic.

I am a marketing consultant. I have worked with many businesses to help them create, execute, and actualize successful e-commerce sites. I hope this book helps you formulate and create your e-commerce direction. I enjoy interacting with interested readers. If you have a question, comment, or success story you would like to share with me, you can visit me on my web site: www.anitarosen.com or write directly to anita@anitarosen.com.

Enjoy!
Anita Rosen

Chapter 1
The Internet Today

Technology, specifically the Internet and e-commerce, is changing the way we do business. This chapter outlines the influences and effects on business today.

Subjects covered in chapter 1

1.1   What is the Internet?

• The Internet provides you with the technical infrastructure to enable an online presence. The Internet is the technical structure enabling people around the world to gain access to the World Wide Web (WWW).

• The Internet can give you the ability to provide present and potential customers, prospects, and business partners easy access to information about your company and products from their home or office.

• Once you obtain a web presence and realize its value, you will be able to offer other goods and services.

Tell Me More

The Internet is a global network made up of smaller networks, linking millions of computers worldwide through the telecommunications infrastructure. The Internet started as a means for researchers and scientists, located in different facilities and in different countries, to share information. The 1990s technical advances, like inexpensive PCs, higher-speed modems (28.8k), browsers (Netscape Communicator and Microsoft Explorer), and easy-to-remember web domain names (www.companyname.com) made the Internet accessible to people outside of the technical community. The Internet provides companies with the technical infrastructure to have a web presence. The WWW resides on top of the Internet; it is the graphical information residing on servers that people access.

It has become apparent that the Internet can provide you with the ability to supply your customers, prospects, and business partners easy access to information about your company and your company's products. Information sharing increases your ability to sell goods and services. Once you have a web presence and realize its value, you will want to look at other offerings you can provide.

1.2   What are first, second, third, and fourth generation web sites?

As use of the Internet became more sophisticated, web sites changed to meet new needs. The changes in the Internet can be categorized in generations of web sites.

   • **Generation One**—Initially companies created simple "brochures-online" web sites.
   • **Generation Two**—As the Internet became more sophisticated, many companies became aware of its potential. Management established web sites that reflected corporate issues: investor relations, company mission statements, and messages from the president.
   • **Generation Three**—As companies began to understand the potential the Internet has for driving business-to-business and business-to-consumer transactions, web sites became simpler, faster, and more focused on specific needs of the person visiting the site.
   • **Generation Four**—The future of the Internet is generation four web sites. Generation four sites physically resemble generation three sites. The difference between generation three and generation four web sites is predominantly behind the scenes. Generation four sites are dynamically created and tightly integrated into the operations of the company.

Tell Me More

Over the last four years, the Internet and its graphical user interface, the WWW, has gone from being a simple marketing and distribution channel to an advanced one. The most drastic changes have been how businesses and consumers use these advances. As companies and users become more sophisticated, the appearance of the Internet changes. Initially companies were satisfied to have a simple presence on the Internet. They took their existing brochures and turned them into online Internet brochures. Since these brochures were created to be distributed on paper, the results of a "brochure online" web site were less than optimal. A brochure online web site is referred to as a **generation one** web site. The signs of a generation one web site are as follows: content tends to be long and difficult to read online, the site is clumsy and difficult to navigate, and it takes a long time to download site information since the graphics were developed for print pieces, so they tend to be very large. On a generation one site, there are few, if any interactive, help, or support features.

As Internet usage grew, most companies changed and updated their web sites. These updated sites became **generation two** web sites. When upper management became aware of a web presence, it tended to push its agenda. Generation two web sites tend to be internally focused. Primary to a generation two web site is information on investor relations, mission statements, job openings, press releases, and messages from the president. These topics are more appropriate for an Intranet (internal) web site or for a limited side-section of a corporate web site. Additionally, generation two web sites tend to be graphically heavy. Graphically heavy features include click-through pages (pages that provide no information, just pretty graphics that the visitor needs to click on to get to information), large product pictures that need to be viewed before the visitor can get product information, and more than one flashing graphic per page. Navigation on generation two sites tends to be cumbersome, since they deny visitors quick access to information. Most visitors find it difficult to go directly to where they want to go. Most web sites are currently generation two web sites.

The current state-of-the-art are **generation three** web sites. You know you are on a generation three site by the use of simple navigation elements, words used for navigation instead of graphics, and content that is focused on the visitor. Most generation three sites use a top and/or side navigation element. This navigation element uses text explanations to download quickly. The home page frames the site in navigation, leaving a center section for changing spotlighted items. Visitors can reach the information in which they are interested within three clicks, without waiting for large graphics to download. Graphics tend to be small, nonanimated, and used to highlight the product. Text is used sparingly: This means it is found in short paragraphs or is bulleted. Internal company information can be found on the site, but it is not spotlighted on the home page.

Generation four web sites are the future of the Internet. Generation four sites resemble generation three sites; the difference is behind the scenes. Generation four sites are tightly integrated into all aspects of the company. When a customer looks for information on a generation four site, the information is generated from a database specifically for that customer. If you go to Amazon.com and perform a search on the word "San Francisco," a listing of all the books with "San Francisco" in the title will be generated and displayed. Behind the scenes, Generation four sites are very sophisticated. Information on a visitor's navigation and buying patterns is maintained and used to update the site. If you go to Dell Computers' web site, you can configure a computer based on your needs by choosing options in a series of pull-down menus. Even if you don't choose to purchase a computer, Dell stores the choices you made. Dell uses this information for market research, specifically to help it identify popular versus unpopular features.

1.3 What is e-commerce?

Electronic commerce or e-commerce covers the range of online business activities for products and services, both business-to-business and business-to-consumer, through the Internet. This section breaks e-commerce into:

- **Online shopping**—the scope of information and activities that provides the customer with the information she needs to conduct business with you and make an informed buying decision.
- **Online purchasing**—the technology infrastructure for the exchange of data and the purchase of a product over the Internet.

It's True: Online purchasing is a metaphor used in business-to-business e-commerce for providing customers with an online method of placing an order, submitting a purchase order, or requesting a quote.

Tell Me More

If you go to a shopping mall to look for a shirt, you may go into several stores. Your shopping experience includes checking the quality, sizes, colors, and prices of different shirts at different stores. Once you have made a decision to buy a shirt, you place it in your shopping cart and continue shopping at that store. When you are done shopping, you take your purchases to the store's cashier. To pay for your transaction, you could provide the cashier with your credit card. E-commerce uses shopping metaphors to define the process of gathering product information and purchasing those products over the Internet. The same metaphors are used for both business-to-business and business-to-consumer transactions. When reviewing products on the Internet, you are **online shopping**. You can place products you are interested in purchasing in your online shopping cart. When you are done shopping and are ready to buy, you can click a purchase button and be moved to an **online purchasing site**. To complete the transaction, you need to supply the online purchasing site with your shipping address and credit card number.

Online shopping provides information and activities that give your customers the knowledge to make informed buying decisions. A consumer who is interested in purchasing a car may research the prices and features of cars online. He may visit the Volkswagen site to find information on the Passat, the Toyota site to learn about the Camry, and the Ford site to investigate the Taurus. He may also visit one of the online car aggregators like www.carpoint.com to get pricing and product information on many different cars. The Internet provides him with an easy way to shop for different products so he can compare features, functionality, and price online. For business-to-business transactions, online shopping may entail an Extranet (private web site) that includes information that business partners may need to conduct business. A manufacturer may provide standard product copy, product pictures, logos, case studies, technical specifications, and product availability on his site. A retailer may go to this site to download a product copy and a graphic for a mailer or newspaper insert. By accessing a business partner's online shopping site, the retailer can be ensured that the picture matches the product and

Staples.com site

Return to Home Page

Shopping Cart 🛒

Subtotal: $3.31
(Just $46.69 to go!)
Free Delivery after $50
View Cart | Check Out

Product Search 🔍

Search by Keyword, Item No.,
Brand, Category...

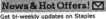

Advanced Search

Find It
Search Help

Time Savers 🕐

· Personalized Lists
· Favorite Aisles
· Quick Order by Item
· Email Reminders
· Past Purchase History
· Product Matchmaker
· Ready Made Lists

News & Hot Offers! ☑

Get bi-weekly updates on Staples
News and Hot Product Offers!
Enter Email Address:

Get It

Earn Rewards $

Small Businesses earn
Staples Dividend$ Dollars

About Staples 📣

· About Staples
· Find a Store
· Request a Catalog
· Apply for Credit
· Job Listings
· Company Info
· Affiliate Program

Customer Service ⓘ

Return to Staples Home

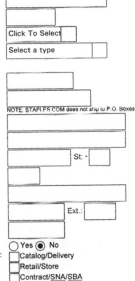

Standard Registration

In order to make a purchase, use our time saving features or simply register, you need to enter your personal, company (if applicable), shipping , delivery, and login information. Once you provide this information, you are a registered user. As a registered user, you will never have to re-enter this information again unless it changes.

After registering, you'll have a personal homepage which presents any time saving features you've chosen to take advantage of (such as personalized lists and email reminders). You will also be able to create new time saving features and change your account information from your personal homepage. Registering at Staples.com only takes a few minutes -- and will save you hours in the long run.

Company Name:

Customer/Dividend Number:

Number of Employees: Click To Select

Type of Business [SIC Code]: Select a type

Billing Address
First Name: ·

Last Name: ·

NOTE: STAPLES.COM does not ship to P.O. Boxes

Address: ·

City: ·   St: ·

Zip: ·

Email Address: ·

Phone: ·   Ext.:

Fax:

Are You An Existing Staples Customer?   ○ Yes ◉ No
If yes, Which Kind? (Check all that apply): ☐ Catalog/Delivery
                                             ☐ Retail/Store
                                             ☐ Contract/SNA/SBA

**Get bi-monthly updates of Staples News
and Hot Product Offers!**
Receive Staples News and Hot Product Offers via e-mail. If you do not want to receive this information please uncheck the box.
Staples News and Hot Product Offers!   ☒

**Submit &
Continue**

· required fields

that the product will be available in the necessary quantities for promotion. Online shopping for business-to-business transactions speeds up the information-gathering and access process, providing timely access to accurate information.

Online purchasing is defined as the infrastructure to allow the purchase of products over the Internet. If a consumer is interested in buying office supplies, she might go to the Staples web site. There she can shop the site, choosing products and placing them in her online shopping basket. When she has found all the products she wants to purchase, she can choose the Staples' online purchasing form to buy the products she has chosen.

A 1998 survey conducted by Zona Research of Redwood City, California, of 100 American companies of over 500 employees, found that 80 percent used the Internet for marketing activities whereas only 10 percent engaged in online purchasing activities. Forty-five percent of the companies surveyed said they planned to implement online purchasing in the next two years.

1.4   How can your company benefit from e-commerce?

The Internet brings you closer to your customer since customers and partners can access information directly. Through the Internet, your company's product information can be accessed directly from the purchaser's desktop. The Internet:

- **Makes the size of a company irrelevant.** Large and small companies have the same access to customers and can create the same kind of Internet presence.
- **Makes the location of a company irrelevant.** Customers located anywhere can easily access your company's site. You can support customers outside of your geographic area.
- **Increases feedback.** You have instantaneous access to your customer responses and feedback when you publish new marketing and pricing programs and new products on your web site.

Tell Me More

The Internet is referred to as a level playing field. Access is based on your web address (www.mycompany.com).

The Internet makes the size of a company irrelevant. Big or small, your company has the same ease of access to potential customers. The web is unlike the real world, where your location and size can affect your ability to access customers. This success is shown by upstarts like Amazon.com, e-trade, and e-toys, all of which have redefined their respective markets and now hold major market share positions on the Internet. These companies did not exist before the Internet. They were able to challenge established companies that had name recognition, established infrastructure, and purchasing power, by having the insight and flexibility to take advantage of this new medium.

Makes the location of a company irrelevant. An advantage of a web presence is that it has no defined location, including time zone and country. Through the web, customers in geographical areas you previously would not have reached can now be accessed easily. Many people visiting your site will be unaware of the size or location of your business. With a web site you can easily support customers located anywhere in the world. Time zones become irrelevant. The Internet is accessible twenty-four hours a day, seven days a week. This access is referred to as a 24×7 web presence. Databases or e-mail typically have interactive features on a web site. Neither databases nor e-mail need human interaction to provide customers with requests for information or services. You can maintain or decrease current staffing while providing current and potential customers with extended hours of support and services. There is no time lag between publishing information on your site and customer access to information. You can track new products and marketing campaigns without delays. Messages, placement, and the focus of your online marketing campaigns can be tweaked at little or no cost and with very little time lag. Additionally, if you have a complete product line and could only get access to shelf space for a segment of it, you can now provide access to all your offerings.

Increases feedback. Most companies have little exposure to their customer's comments and feedback. This is especially true of companies that conduct business-to-business transactions without direct access to their end-user customer. The Internet's interactive qualities and easy access provide companies with direct information. A tool as simple as a "contact us" button on a web site can give customers an easy way to provide a company with feedback. Additionally, news and discussion groups can provide a company with insight into the general market or a specific product. If your company sells stereo equipment, you can go to a stereo discussion group and see what subjects are of interest to people, or what they are saying about your or your competitors' products, providing you with a window into the consumer's mind.

1.5   Can small companies compete with big companies?

E-commerce makes it easy for companies to provide customers with a worldwide presence.

- The Internet tends to yield profits to both small and large companies.
- An Internet presence is easy to establish for both small and large companies.
- Because of a more level playing field, the Internet is proportionally more advantageous for smaller companies.
- A small company's flexible, innovative management style provides a competitive advantage in the ever-changing world of the Internet.

Tell Me More

Due to the more level playing field on the web, small companies that build sites can generate as much revenue as larger companies. Relatively speaking, a million dollars of revenue could double the profits of a small company, but be considered insignificant by a large company.

Small companies that have grasped the Internet e-commerce paradigm have benefited with a growing market share. Larger companies have often only sought the benefits of an e-commerce site when a small, unknown business has taken market share away from the larger business. On the Internet, a professional-looking site is relatively easy to build and maintain. A small business using the Internet as its chief distribution channel provides quick support and innovative services. It is easier for a small company to change its internal infrastructure to adapt to the new needs of on-line commerce. Large companies, which tend to have slower, more bureaucratic structures, are at a disadvantage. As the Internet grows and changes the face of business, large companies will need to change their internal infrastructures to provide flexible systems to support the demands of the Internet.

1.6 What is an Extranet site?

An Extranet provides you with an Internet site that is accessible to a select group of people.

- An Extranet provides you with the ability to create applications that associates and customers can access, but that are not accessible to the general public.
- Extranets can use encryption and password protection to secure access to the site.
- For business-to-business transactions, Extranets enable secure electronic commerce.
- An Extranet can automate information sharing by providing access to specific information and controlled access to internal databases.

Tell Me More

An Internet site provides you with a web presence for the general public. An Intranet site uses Internet technology to provide your employees with access to internal information. An Extranet provides you with an Internet site accessible to a select group of people.

In an Extranet site, existing customers and partners are given password-protected access to information pertinent to them. Partners and customers can access this information whereas the general public cannot. Extranets can use encryption and password technologies to secure access to your site. For business-to-business transactions, Extranets can enable secure electronic commerce. An Extranet can automate information sharing by providing access to specific information and regulated access to internal databases.

Within an Extranet site, you can create a location for disseminating nondisclosure information. You can simultaneously host many Extranet services, each focused on the needs of one particular constituency. For example, existing customers who have purchased from different product lines may have access to an Extranet service focused on their needs. Business partners may have access to a partner's Extranet site that has information on pricing, sales promotions, or other personalized services. Investors may have access to an Extranet site with financial information or discounts specifically for them. Each Extranet site may share access to your company's e-commerce application. You can specify different products or provide discounts based on Extranet or user passwords.

A company that manufactures pharmaceuticals may have a web site that consumers can visit to learn more about some popular off-the-shelf products. The site may include recent tests, use practices, recommendations, and side-effect warnings. The company may also create an Extranet site for its sales staff. Sales reps need to know the unpublished location of this site and have a pin number to access the information. Once on the Extranet site, sales reps can place orders, track their customers' ordering trends, find out information about sales incentives, and obtain competitive information. Doctors may be given access to a different Extranet site. On the doctors' Extranet site, the company may run discussion groups for doctors who have used the product, provide clinical trial results, and run specials for buying online.

1.7   How does the Internet affect the way we work?

The Internet is changing the way people work.

- **Digitization**—Employees now have the ability to store many types of information on a computer.
- **Globalization**—The Internet provides a global community: Employees and partners may be located anywhere.
- **Mobility**—Employees now have access to information wherever they go.
- **Workgroups**—Employees from different locations can collaborate on projects.

- **Immediacy**—Employees can have real-time access to information wherever they are.

Tell Me More

The Internet is changing the way people work.

Digitization—Any information that can be digitized can be stored and retrieved by a computer, thus increasing access to information; there is no need for human intervention. If a company has an archive of videos used for commercials, it can digitize and store these commercials on a central video server. If an employee located anywhere in an advertising office wants to view an ad campaign from two years ago, she no longer needs to call up an employee from the central storage office to order a videotape. She can now access the video server through the company's Intranet and play the video on the PC in her office.

Globalization—The Internet provides companies with the infrastructure to provide their partners and employees with access to information, regardless of where they are physically. Previously, employees needed to be located near information in order to access it.

Mobility—Internet technology provides a person with the ability to access information wherever he is. Employees can now have the same access to information if they are working out of their homes or working at their offices. Employees who need to travel to support customers are no longer constrained by the inability to access information that resides within the company. Access to information from any place and at any time can improve the company's ability to respond to customer needs.

Workgroups—Internet technology supports data sharing and employee collaboration. Project information and interactive conversations can now be hosted on a computer. Companies can create joint development teams where members of the team can reside in different geographic areas. Collaboration tools such as newsgroups, chat groups, and bulletin boards can be used so members of the groups can post comments and communicate with each other.

Immediacy—People can have real-time access to information, no matter what time of day or night it is. By accessing a web site, a partner's Extranet, or the company's Intranet, the latest price, configuration, or ship date can be found instantly by the person who needs this information.

1.8   What is disintermediation?

Disintermediation is the process of becoming closer to your customer by eliminating the middleman.

- **Time**—When your company automates procedures, time may be the middleman that is being disintermediated.
- **People**—Automation of procedures can disintermediate people currently handling the procedures.
- **Distribution channels**—Providing an online purchasing site can disintermediate an existing distribution channel.

It's True: Intermediation is the process of creating a new middleman; online auction house eBay is an intermediator.

Tell Me More

Time, people, and distribution channels can be disintermediated. By providing customers, partners, and employees with direct access to information, you can provide them with complete control to request and receive information.

Time can be disintermediated by automating a procedure. Automating processes and providing people with Internet tools to access those processes can save time.

If your company's current ordering procedures include employing a clerk to input the order, automating these procedures can disintermediate **people**.

A manufacturer who has never sold directly to the public may decide to open up an online sales purchasing site. This online purchasing site can provide direct sales, disintermediating a **distribution channel**.

By providing customers, partners, or employees direct access to information, the information middleman is eliminated. Previously a customer needed to fax in an order, then wait for a sales representative to call back with the availability dates of the items. The customer can now place an order directly by using an Extranet site. As the customer places the order, the Extranet site displays availability dates for the different items. If the customer sees that an item has too long a lead time, he can substitute the item for one with a shorter lead time. With direct access to information, a customer does not have to wait for sales representative availability.

It is interesting to note that in some instances, the Internet has created **intermediation**. Intermediation is the opposite of disintermediation: It is the adding of an intermediary to facilitate business. EBay, the online auction house, is an example of intermediation. EBay has no product, stock, or inventory. People with something to sell register their item with eBay. People interested in buying a product go to the ebay site to see what products are for sale. Without a service like eBay, it would be very difficult for buyers and sellers to come together. EBay adds an intermediary to the process of buying and selling goods.

1.9   How has the Internet enabled companies to move from mass marketing to mass customization?

The Internet provides companies with the infrastructure to participate in the paradigm shift.

- You can move from providing general information or products to providing information or products customized to your visitors' needs.
- To provide mass customization, two technologies are used:
  —**Push technology:** The seeker is automatically provided with information by being sent to the right place. This is similar to television, where the broadcaster sends information over the airwaves and the consumer chooses the channel of his or her choice.
  —**Pull technology:** The seeker must express a need in order to receive information. This is similar to an ATM, where the consumer inputs her password and then receives account information specified by her.

Tell Me More

Previously, companies had focused their marketing efforts on market segmentation and mass marketing to these segments. The new trend, mass customization, uses Internet tools to create services where customers and partners can identify their preferences and a web site can serve them information tailored to their needs. Dolls that are sold with different skin pigmentation are an example of mass marketing to market segments. This approach provides you with the ability to focus your product on individual characteristics of a group of people, providing you with a unique product tailored specifically to individuals who should in return increase market share and profits.

The Internet provides you with the infrastructure to take part in the current marketing paradigm shift, mass customization. It gives visitors to your site the tools to customize the information you provide to their needs. These tools might be as complex as a form that interfaces with a database, to an e-mail that is automatically generated based on conditions specified by the visitor.

The Barbie site

Mattel's Barbie Doll division has used mass customization on its web site to provide a new and unique product. The Internet provides it with an easy, accessible user interface for this new custom service. Previously, Mattel only mass marketed its dolls. It manufactured dolls with different skin tones, hair colors, and clothing based on generic demographic sampling. With mass customization Mattel can provide a customer to its site with a unique doll. Customers can choose between a selection of doll characteristics including skin tone, eye color, hair color, hairstyle, and clothing. They can personalize the doll with a unique name. After the customer makes the selection, the site displays a graphic of what the doll will look like. The customer can then modify any of the components. Once the customer is satisfied, he can order the doll online. The Barbie division has backed up this web application with a powerful database that is tightly integrated with a new manufacturing line specifically designed to create and ship individually configured dolls. It took the Barbie division of Mattel two years to develop and implement the manufacturing line for this new product. Mattel had been in the early planning stage of providing a mass-customized product. The company thought that the Internet would be an ideal vehicle for providing a mass-customized service.

Mass customization comes in two forms: push and pull. **Pull** technology is dependent on information that is specified by the visitor. The visitor pulls information from the web site. Most web sites are based on pull technology. The person specifies what site he or she wants to go to by entering a destination in the URL (web address [www.companyname.com]). The site is then available to the person who requested the information. A popular form of pull is using a data entry screen. The customers or partners select options that are of interest to them. A new web page is generated and displayed based on this criteria, making it easy for them to find information.

The Custom Barbie Doll site is an example of pull technology. So is Federal Express. If you are sending a package from one location to another via Federal Express, you go to the Federal Express web site, input your destination country and air-bill tracking number, and receive information on when your package will arrive.

This is a convenient way for customers to access custom information.

Push technology is also a way of providing clients with mass-customized information. It is information sent directly to customers and partners by the web site's server. A television transmission is a good example of push technology. In a television transmission, the broadcaster sends information over the airwaves and the consumer chooses the channel of his choice. Push technology is referred to as an event-driven technology. A consumer may set up stock price parameters with his financial institution. The consumer fills out an online form specifying that if a stock price falls or rises beyond a specified mark, the financial institution is to notify him.

The same push technology can be used to notify different customers about different kinds of events. A manufacturing company may use push technology to notify a customer if a part is shipped, or a sports service may use push technology to give a sports fan the score of a game.

E-mail is a popular notification tool for push technology. Companies send or push e-mail to customers and partners who subscribe to a particular mailing list. E-mail mailing lists can supply customers and partners with information on product enhancements, pricing specials, or support bulletins. Customers and partners can sign up for a mailing list on a web site by adding their names to that mailing list. For the stock market, a customer fills out a form detailing the stocks in which she is interested and the minimum and maximum prices. The customer-defined information in the form is placed in a database. When the stock reaches the specified minimum or maximum, the database automatically creates an e-mail notifying the customer of the event.

The financial institution can also activate sales tools to coincide with push technology events. On the bottom of the e-mail page, the financial institution may include a hyperlinked web address (URL). When the address is clicked, the customer is brought to a web screen, where she is asked to input her personal identification number (PIN). Once the pin is verified, the customer's profile information is automatically displayed and the customer can execute an order.

The Internet supports the integration of multiple types of electronic devices. By integrating web technology with pagers, companies can push real-time information to their subscribers. Pager notification can be used when time-critical information needs to be sent to a customer who has limited computer access, but twenty-four-hour access to a pager (i.e., pagernumber@skytel.com). A financial institution can send an e-mail notification to a customer's pager. The customer may be playing golf, but he will still be notified of a buy or sell opportunity. Or a manufacturing company can notify its customer who is working in the field that a critical part has left the factory. This is an efficient way to provide specifically customized services to your customers.

1.10   What are the current media myths about the Internet?

The media have done numerous reports on perceived shortcomings of doing business over the Internet. You will hear about the following shortcomings of doing business on the Internet:

- Hackers can get access to my personal information.
- Commerce doesn't work on the Internet.
- Transactions are not safe.

Tell Me More

Since the explosion of the Internet, there have been many stories about the unmet expectations of commerce over the Internet, risks of transacting business over the Internet, and the abilities of hackers to get access to personal information. Since most businesses are concerned with both the real and perceived benefits and deficits of doing business over the Internet, it is wise to understand the realities of the perceived risks.

1.11   Can Internet transactions and communications be secure?

Security is a very important issue for companies doing business on the Internet. There are many reliable technologies available today to make Internet transactions safe for your business.

- By developing a site that uses secure server transactions, you can protect your company and your customers when buying online.
- Internet credit card transactions are generally safer than telephone credit card sales, as long as they are encrypted.
- Encryption ensures that if a transaction is intercepted, it is unreadable.
- You should not create an e-commerce site unless you deploy secure server and encryption technology.

Tell Me More

It is true that transactions over the Internet can be intercepted and read by intruders; however, it is also true that transactions over the Internet can be made safe. There are a variety of reliable technologies available to make Internet transactions safe for business.

The most popular technology used to make e-mail safe is encryption. Encryption changes the characters of the transmission so they are unreadable unless you have a decryption key. If you want to send an e-mail over the Internet and you want to make sure that the only party who can read the e-mail is the recipient, you can provide the recipient with a keyword. Then, in a separate e-mail, you can send them the message. The recipient can decrypt the message by entering the keyword into the decryption software program. If an intruder intercepts the e-mail, he will be unable to read the message without the keyword. Encryption is a reliable and safe method of sending information over the Internet. An encrypted transaction over the Internet works the same way as encrypting an e-mail. The difference is that servers and browsers come with an encryption program. This way, the keyword is sent and received without human intervention.

Encryption is one element of secure server technology for transmitting credit card information over the Internet. A secure server automatically includes encryption functionality. The customer's browser sends and receives the decryption key, automating the process of sending, receiving, and entering an encryption key.

An educated online consumer knows that he should only send credit card information over a secure server. Netscape users know they are on a secure server when the key symbol in the lower left-hand corner of the screen is no longer broken. Microsoft users know they are on a secure server when the lock in the lower right-hand corner of the screen of their browser turns blue and the key or lock symbol is no longer broken.

No one should provide credit card information over the Internet on anything but a secure server. You should educate your customers on the risks of sending personal information over a non-secure server compared to the safety of sending information over a secure server. Chapter three goes into greater depth on secure server and encryption technologies.

1.12 Are companies really making money on their e-commerce sites?

Many companies are just beginning to use the Internet for commerce. Newspapers are full of stories of Internet companies that have billion-dollar market capitalization and have not yet made a profit. The reality is:

- Many companies have successful e-commerce sites.
- Since the technology is new, people are conservative when purchasing over the Internet. The financial rewards of doing business transactions over the Internet are growing fast.
- You will need to integrate e-commerce into your overall marketing and sales strategy to make it lucrative.

Tell Me More

The media have been quick to note that some companies have not met their financial expectations with electronic commerce and that many Internet start-ups are not operating in the black. In reality, many companies have created successful electronic commerce sites. Successful technology companies have been at the forefront of creating online shopping and purchasing sites for both business-to-business and business-to-consumer transactions. Two companies that have successfully used the Internet to sell their products are Dell and Cisco. Dell is generating more than seven million dollars a day in web sales, while Cisco exceeded one billion dollars in annual sales over the web in 1998.

For companies that have not integrated marketing, operations, and technology into the way they do business, e-commerce has been slower than predicted for generating business.

It takes time for a company to understand and manage e-commerce as a new business channel, instead of viewing it as a brochure-like technology and marketing tool. A manufacturer might not have the infrastructure to tie its web site into the current applications. Online purchasing includes a financial transaction and the need to fill an order. These transactions create the need for accounting, inventory control, shipping, and customer service to get involved with the creation of an e-commerce site.

Early reports based on Fortune 2000 companies skew the picture of future success of the Internet. Many large companies expected that by creating a web site and including online purchasing, they would instantaneously create a major source of revenue. Like any other distribution channel, developing a successful e-commerce service requires a considerable amount of time, energy, and initiative. We will discuss many ways companies can integrate e-commerce into their business practices and create successful channels for doing business.

Internet business technology is new, which is an additional hindrance. Tools that manage web sites are immature, making it difficult for new web managers to integrate services. Business on the Internet is still in its infancy. Businesses are just beginning to explore how an Internet presence will help them conduct business. Most analysts see e-commerce as an emerging and growing business channel. According to CommerceNet, a consortium for developing commerce on the Internet, in the United States in 1997, about thirty million web users shopped online, while around ten million purchased online. By the year 2000, they predict that in the United States, almost ninety million people will be shopping online, while nearly forty million will be purchasing online.

At Pricewaterhouse Coopers World Economic Forum, 35 percent of companies around the world said they expected to get no e-business trade in 1999, while only 8 percent expected to get no e-business trade by 2004.

To maximize the benefits of online shopping and purchasing,

Graph showing the growth of commerce over the Internet

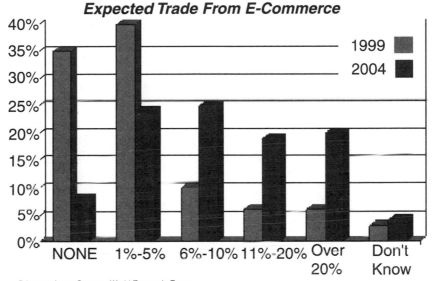

Expected Trade From E-Commerce

PricewaterhouseCoopers, World Economic Forum

you will need to integrate e-commerce into your overall marketing and sales strategy and integrate this strategy with your operations and information services organizations. Integrating e-commerce will actively change how you do business. Your accounting department will need to monitor e-commerce transactions; your sales organization will need to train customers to use your web site; operations will need to adjust so it can fulfill online transactions; and marketing will need to develop programs that play well on the Internet. Integrating your e-commerce site with your direction includes making sure product information on your web site is updated on a timely basis. Any document that would include your company's phone number should also include your company's web address. This includes business cards, letterhead, advertisements, data sheets, and invoices. E-commerce is not a separate marketing function, but a distribution channel that needs to be integrated into the fabric of your company.

1.13   Is it possible to stop hackers?

There are many successful strategies for companies to provide security to their web sites.

- There is a low probability that a hacker is targeting you or your company.
- Hackers tend to go after big name companies and organizations. They are often looking for recognition from other hackers.
- Companies that use currently accepted methods of safeguarding their technology assets probably will not be affected by hackers.
- Hackers usually cannot affect transactions that are being conducted using a secure server.

Tell Me More

Since the Internet is built on a loosely connected network of millions of computers providing easy access to anyone, security of information can be difficult to ensure. If you are concerned with the security of transactions or with intruders having access to private information, there are many successful strategies available to provide security for your web site.

Since there is a tremendous amount of information on the Internet, there is a low probability that a hacker is targeting you or your company. Hackers tend to go after big name companies and organizations. They are usually looking for recognition from other hackers. Organizations that are high-level targets are the military and financial institutions. If you work at a company or organization that would be a target for hackers, your Information Systems department should provide your organization with many advanced security features. Many companies have chosen to host their entire web site, including their e-commerce site, on their ISP's server. Transactions are downloaded periodically to a computer at the company. This way, hackers have no access to the company's internal computers.

If your internal computer networks access the Internet, there is no 100 percent secure way to safeguard yourself from a dedicated hacker. Hackers should not affect companies that use state-of-the-art, currently accepted methods of safeguarding their technology assets (e.g., hosting Internet accounts on a mutually exclusive network and using password protection, secure servers, firewalls, and routers). If your company is performing transactions over the Internet, hackers should not be able to read those transactions provided you are using a secure server. Another strategy companies can use to protect important e-mail sent outside the company includes providing employees with e-mail encryption tools.

Locating company information on a mutually exclusive network and on separate web servers from the company's Internet web site are necessary steps to provide protection from intruders. Technology like firewalls must be used to safeguard company servers that have access to the Intranet. Firewalls are computers that work like security guards. They separate the external network from the internal network, while allowing a bridge so employees can receive e-mail and access the Internet from their workstations. Firewalls also scan files entering the company for viruses and have many technical deterrents to keep intruders from getting inside the company's network.

The greatest breach in company security usually comes from the inside. Disgruntled employees can cause much more havoc to a company than an outside intruder. Creating internal backup systems and limiting internal access to systems by password protection are the best safeguards to internal threats.

1.14 Chapter summary

The Internet has exploded on the business landscape over the last few years, and it has changed the course of business.

- Over the last few years, businesses have begun to learn how to use this new resource to expand their market reach.
- The look and capabilities of web sites have changed as businesses have become more sophisticated at using the Internet as a business tool.
- What has become evident is that the Internet provides an

opportunity for all companies, regardless of their size, to interface with customers, disintermediating time, people, and processes.
• This provides companies with the opportunity to increase their services by providing mass customization.

Chapter 2
Identifying Your Direction

This chapter will help you to create successful e-commerce services by helping you to understand the effect of e-commerce on your company, customers, and business partners.

Subjects covered in chapter 2

2.1   Is your product a good candidate for e-commerce?

2.2   Is your service a good candidate for e-commerce?

2.3   What are e-commerce strategies for use-based services?

2.4   What is online account reconciliation?

2.5   Is online shopping right for your company?

2.6   How will your customers respond to your e-commerce services?

2.7   What are the basic elements of an online shopping service?

2.8   How will your distributors respond to e-commerce?

2.9   How can your online shopping site affect your business partners?

2.10 What is online procurement and how does it work?

2.11 What tools can you develop to support customers, distributors, and partners?

2.12 Will your company's infrastructure support the implementation and growth of e-commerce?

2.13 Will your company change when you integrate e-commerce into your business direction?

2.14 Chapter summary

2.1   Is your product a good candidate for e-commerce?

The first step in building an e-commerce site is determining whether your goods are appropriate to be sold over the Internet.

- The most obvious products to sell over the Internet are recognizable commodities or brand name products.
- If a product is easily available in the marketplace, there must be some additional and compelling reason for someone to want to purchase the product from a web site.
- If your product is for a niche market, the decisive reason to sell it over the Internet may be the access to a broader market.
- If your company has created an international or regional reputation, you should use this reputation to expand your market when selling over the Internet.
- Be sure that there are no legal limitations to selling your product over the Internet.

Tell Me More

The most obvious products to sell over the Internet are commodity or brand name products. Commodity products are those the customers understand and thus know what they are getting, sight unseen, even if they have never heard of the manufacturer. PCs are a good example of a commodity. A PC manufacturer can provide the specifications and list components (i.e., Intel Pentium processor, Microsoft operating system) of its PC and the customer can understand the product's functionality and quality.

A brand name instantly identifies the manufacturer and quality of the product. Coca-Cola and McDonald's are instantly recognized brand names found all around the world. Books are brand name products that are currently being sold over the Internet. Books contain a publisher's brand name and an author's brand name. Consumers going to a new web site would not question, and can instantly identify, the quality of a Robert Ludlum book published by Bantam.

If a product is easily available in the marketplace, there must be additional, compelling reasons for someone to want to purchase it from a web site. Peapod.com is a site that sells groceries on the Internet (www.peapod.com). Since grocery stores are easily found in most neighborhoods, for Peapod.com to succeed, it has to provide an experience that is better than that of shopping at the local grocery store. Peapod has created advantageous services through online ordering and home delivery. Customers who are interested in these services find Peapod a compelling market.

Other companies use an e-commerce site to go after unusual or specialized markets. The Internet lets them expand their market reach. Headroom is a manufacturer of high-end headphones. Headroom has a web site, www.headphone.com, through which it sells its headphones over the Internet. The headphones it manufactures and sells are typically not found at most audio stores. Audiophiles who are interested in high-end headphones will search out a specialized product like theirs. Consumers who are interested in high-end headphones are a small, geographically dispersed, but sophisticated group. Headroom has found that an online presence has provided it with access to a market that it would have had a difficult time identifying and servicing with a retail store.

Customers may question the unseen quality and legitimacy of buying a product over the Internet from a company they do not know. They may doubt that a product purchased from an unknown web site will be delivered to their home or office. If your product does not fit into the commodity or brand name category, or your company is not well known, you will need to provide supporting information to your customer so that he can understand the quality and trust that you will deliver the product.

Companies that have created an international or regional reputation can use this reputation to expand their market when selling over the Internet. A customer buying a product from an international company like Disney, or a company located in select regions like Macy's, may already be familiar with the company's image and trust it. When purchasing from a known company, consumers feel confident the product will actually be delivered.

Understanding a product's legal limitations is necessary when creating an e-commerce site. Due to state laws, real estate companies in the United States cannot sell beyond their state lines. This limits the information that can be displayed on an online shopping site. A real estate company selling a planned community can provide potential buyers with information on the property, an online tour of the homes, statistics on the community, and information on amenities and services, but it cannot provide an online prospectus. The goal of an online shopping site for a real estate company that is marketing to potential customers in other states would be to provide them with enough information to spark their interest. The online shopping service goal would be to generate leads that would be followed up by local realtors.

Here are a few basic questions that you will need to answer in order to evaluate whether your product is appropriate for online e-commerce. A "no" answer does not mean your product is not appropriate for e-commerce; it just highlights where you must place extra emphasis when developing your e-commerce site.

Questionnaire for Companies Selling Products Over the Internet

Yes / No	Question	Response
	Is your product easy for people to understand sight unseen?	Yes—You should be straightforward when explaining it on your web site. No—You will need additional material to provide potential customers with information on your product.
	Is your product or company a brand or known name?	Yes—You can use your known name to provide potential customers with the security that they are buying from a reputable company. No—Provide money back offers and references to make potential customers feel comfortable (e.g., provide a list of known customers, provide positive press articles on your company, provide customer testimonials).

Yes	Question	Response
No		
	Can you clearly identify the demographics of the people who buy your product?	Yes—Identify demographics and customer need to create an online shopping site and advertise your product using niche portals. No—Do market research. If your market segment is very large, define a smaller initial market segment.
	Would people find it more convenient to buy your product from their desk at home or in their office rather than over the phone, fax, or in person?	Yes—Build an online purchasing site. No—You can use your site to provide customers with product information and customer service.
	Are you capable of reaching your potential market? Are there people who would buy your product if they could get access to a distribution channel?	Yes—You already have a good distribution channel. You can use e-commerce to augment this channel and provide any easy-to-access service for your customers. No—You can expand your market reach and services by providing e-commerce services.
	Is it legal for you to sell your products directly to consumers and businesses from a web site?	Yes—You can use your site to close business through an online purchasing service. No—Your site can be focused on providing product information, customer support, and customer service.

2.2 Is your service a good candidate for e-commerce?

Selling services over the Internet is similar to selling products.

To sell services over the Internet, you must be able to adequately explain your service online.

- The best services for e-commerce do not require personal interaction, such as those found in construction, car detailing, personal delivery, or alarm installation.
- If your service requires personal interaction with a customer, you can still have a successful e-commerce site by limiting the site to a geographic area.
- There needs to be a compelling reason for people to purchase your service over the Internet.
- Documents need to be created so that there are records of all transactions.

Tell Me More

The two most popular and lucrative items currently being sold over the Internet are services: airplane tickets and financial services like stocks and bonds. Microsoft's largest online revenue from non-software-based business is its air-ticketing service, Expedia, located at www.expedia.com. New companies like E-Trade, and established brokerage firms like Charles Schwab, are changing the nature of individual investing. In 1999, one in every six share trades takes place over the Internet. Brokerage firms and financial institutions selling over the Internet have created very sophisticated web sites. They have affected international stock markets by creating day traders. They have had a profound impact on the cost of trading, driving prices of a tradedown from $100 to $15. Do you want to see the latest in financial sites? Visit www.quicken.com to get an up-to-date listing provided by Morningstar on any publicly traded company. Using online purchasing can be an effective and influential method to access service-based customers.

If you currently have a service-based company and want to sell your services over the Internet, you will have to be sure that your service can be explained and sold online. In most situations, an e-commerce site that includes online shopping and online purchasing will work best if the service does not require personal interaction.

An alarm installation company can explain its services, take orders, and service existing customers. However, the alarm company will have a hard time installing an alarm outside of its geographic area. If a service-based company needs physical interaction with a customer, it can create an online shopping site that can limit the support based on geographic considerations. The easiest way to limit access to an online shopping site is to have customers enter their zip code or area code. If a zip code or area code is not within the company's geographic area, the web site can display a message thanking the customer and informing him that the company does not provide services to the visitors' region. Peapod provides a regional grocery delivery service. Peapod first asks a potential customer for his zip code. If he enters a New York zip code, he will be taken to a screen that explains that it does not provide service in his area and that asks him to provide information on his location for future reference.

The principles we discussed for selling products over the Internet also apply to selling services. Is your service specialized or hard to find in some areas? If so, the Internet may provide you with a wider distribution channel. Is it more convenient for a cus-

Limiting service from your web site

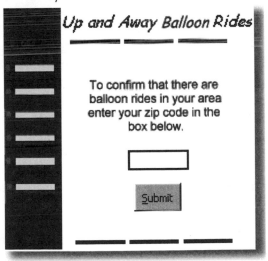

Up and Away Balloon Rides

To confirm that there are balloon rides in your area enter your zip code in the box below.

Submit

tomer to purchase your service online instead of going to a store? If so, an e-commerce site will also work for you. Can you provide better services over the Internet than you can in a face-to-face situation? Many financial institutions have found they can. For example, financial service customers can access their personal portfolios on a financial institution's site and play an online game of "What if" scenarios. If you have invested $100,000 in a specific financial institution's fund and it has an interactive web site, you can see what would happen if you diversified your portfolio by choosing other funds. You can even view projected rates of return versus projected risks. Additionally, you can project how much money you will have in your retirement account based on your level of risk and your savings rate.

Online stock trading has become a popular use of the Internet. Financial institutions that sell stocks and bonds over the Internet provide customers with stock and bond tracking services and the ability to trade online. They believe that by providing their customers with access to powerful analyzing, forecasting, and event notification software, they are providing them with a positive experience. When customers are informed, they can access tools to project the future performance of their assets in different scenarios. They will thus be more likely to purchase additional services.

When you sell services over the Internet, you will need to provide your customers with documents confirming that the transaction took place, since your customer will not be expecting to receive a tangible product. With a plane ticket, your customers may receive an e-mail order confirmation before the plane tickets are mailed to them. If you are a financial institution and a customer orders a financial service, you can send the customer an e-mail confirming the order. If people purchase a service over the Internet, they need to feel that the company from which they are buying provides a good, legitimate service. A company like Fidelity Investments or Charles Schwab has a well-known name and an existing service organization to augment online sales. Small regional companies can to comarket their services with a known entity or obtain positive write-ups to help customers feel safe and secure.

Here are a few basic questions that you will need to answer in order to figure out if your **service** is appropriate for online e-commerce. A "no" answer does not mean your service is not appropriate for e-commerce; it just highlights where you must place extra emphasis when developing your site.

Questionnaire for Companies Selling Services Over the Internet

Yes / No	Question	Response
	Is your service a commodity that is easy for people to understand site unseen?	Yes—Should be straightforward. No—Will need additional material to provide potential customers with information on your product.
	Is your service or company a brand or known name?	Yes—You can use your known name to provide potential customers with the security that they are buying from a reputable company. No—You will need to give references (i.e., provide a list of customers, positive press articles on your company, or customer testimonials).
	Can you clearly identify the demographics of the people who buy your product?	Yes—Identify demographics and customer needs to create an online shopping site and advertise your product using niche portals. No—Do more market research. If your market segment is very large, define a smaller initial market segment.
	Are you reaching your potential market? Are there people who would buy your service if they could get access to a distribution channel?	Yes—You already have a good distribution channel. You can use e-commerce to augment this channel and provide any easy-to-access service for your customers.

(continued)

Yes / No	Question	Response
		No—You can expand your market reach and services by providing e-commerce services.
	Would people find it more convenient to buy your service from their desk at home or in their office than over the phone, fax, or in person?	Yes—Build an online purchasing site. No—You can use your site to provide customers with product information and customer service.
	Is your service physically limited (i.e., do you need to deploy people to install/ provide your service)?	Yes—You can still build an online purchasing site; you will need to limit access of your service based on zip code or area code. No—Your service is a good candidate for online purchasing.
	Is it legal for you to sell your service directly to consumers and businesses from a web site over state or country lines?	Yes—Your service is a good candidate for online purchasing. No—You can use your site for online shopping and to provide customer support service.

2.3   What are e-commerce strategies for use-based services?

Many companies provide a service that is being used continuously. These companies may also be good candidates for e-commerce.

- Companies with a use-fee are typically utility companies (telephone, gas, electric, garbage, and sewer), apartment houses, or banks.

- Use-based service suppliers can offer an online shopping site to better serve existing customers and to provide customers with information on new and existing services.
- If you are a use-fee service supplier, an online shopping and purchasing site can become a convenient and cost-saving addition to the way you are currently doing business.
- A use-fee service supplier can use online purchasing for bill payments and for simplifying and automating the billing system.

Tell Me More

Many companies have products that are continually being used by customers. Existing customers pay an access or use-fee. An example of an access or use-fee is a phone bill, electric bill, or cable TV bill. Companies with a use-fee are typically utilities like telephone, gas, electricity, cable TV, and garbage collection. Other types of businesses with a use-fee are apartment houses and banks. Most use-based service companies are established businesses with a broad consumer base. Utility customers are familiar with their current use-for-pay billing system. Consumers are looking for ways to consolidate, simplify, and manage their budgets.

If your company is service oriented, you may want to create an online shopping and online purchasing service focused on convenience. That way, you entice customers to learn more about your services, teach them better ways to use your service, and lead them to buy additional services.

Service suppliers find an online purchasing site a better way to manage their costs. Use-based service companies are looking for ways to streamline business practices while maintaining service levels. Online billing is a method of providing new convenience-based services that benefit both the company and the consumer. By providing consumers with direct access to their bills, service companies can automate the process of sending out bills and processing payments, saving time for consumers and employees. Automating bill payments cuts costs (since fewer people are needed to process payments), increases cash flow (since money is electronically received), and provides better services (since consumers can access better bill management tools). Additionally, service suppliers can use mass customization online shopping and purchasing services to provide existing customers with information on existing and newly customized services for individuals based on their use patterns.

2.4   What is online account reconciliation?

Online account statements can provide customers with accurate, up-to-date information that can increase services while cutting costs.

- Service companies can provide their customers with an on-line statement, cutting their mailing and processing costs while increasing their range of services.
- Online statements can include interactive tools so customers can better understand and manage the services they are purchasing.
- Service companies can provide add-on services based on a customer's use pattern. This addition can increase customer satisfaction, improve services, and create additional sales.

Tell Me More

For most use-based companies, the bill is the brand. Most consumers don't think about their electric company every time they turn on a light. The only time consumers think about a utility is when there is a power outage or when they receive their electric bill.

Typically, the bill is the only chance the service provider has to communicate with the consumer. Many service providers use the bill to provide consumers with information about their services or to cross sell additional services. Enlightened service providers look at billing as sales and customer-bonding opportunities, not just as the collection of receivables. An online shopping site can take this bonding opportunity a step further, because an online electronic bill can be used to draw a customer into a regular inter-active electronic dialogue with her service provider.

Use-based service providers can cut costs and yield higher profits by using online billing. The cost savings from reduced paper processing are estimated to be somewhere between $0.75 and $1.25 for each paper check that is eliminated. Service providers also gain by decreasing the float of the money, since they are no longer dealing with the time it takes to process paper, cancelled checks, or bad checks. Customers can also be ensured of remembering to pay their bill on time, because they can ask their service provider to send them e-mail reminders before the bill is due.

Another reason for use-based services to create their own online billing system is the growing trend for bill consolidation. Bill consolidators are a consumer financial service. Consumers sign up for this service through their financial institutions and the bill consolidator automatically pays a consumer's bill. Bill consolidators intermediate (become the information middleman) between a utility company and the customer. In an unregulated environment, most utility companies view direct access to the customer as a precious commodity. Some service providers are designing electronic billing and payment receipt processes to avoid bill consolidators, thus enhancing their own branded, one-to-one, direct interaction with their customers. Online payment systems not only provide the customer with added information about their bills but provide easy payment options like online credit card payment or direct transfer of money from the customer's bank account. Many customers are reluctant to lose control of paying bills by using automatic payment systems. An online payment system can provide customers with added features and more control of the process.

How Does This Work?

A presentment is the statement most people currently receive from their utility company. A service supplier can provide its customers with online account reconciliation that allows them to view and pay their bills online. Service providers can display a presentment on the online purchasing component of their web site. Creating an online presentment involves taking the statement data that are currently being mailed to a customer and hosting that information on an interactive online shopping server. An advantage to your customer from online presentment is that he can pay bills online and can customize the information he receives. An electric utility company provides customers with last-year-this-time and current-use figures. Online, it can provide a tool by which customers can display use patterns for the past twenty-four months, helping its users identify where they have spikes in usage.

Kansas City Power and Light (KCPL) is an electric utility company currently providing its customers with online billing services. Due to deregulation in the power industry, they feel that they need to provide customers with new services and options. KCPL sees online billing and account management as a means of providing proactive services. Regulatory agencies have denied them the ability to let customers who receive online bills opt not to receive paper bills. In the future, KCPL hopes to overcome regulatory issues and provide customers with the online-only option, simplifying the billing process for customers and saving them from printing and mailing bills.

KCPL consumers can pay their bills and view their payment histories, current bills, current usage, and usage histories online. Commercial customers have additional options. They can view their bills and sort usage based on a number of options they define themselves. Customers are very positive about the service. The most popular feature has been the graph that displays usage. In the future, KCPL would like to offer online customers the option to set their payment date, pay by credit card, and register for e-mail payment reminders.

Internet bill presentment and payment options can be used to create cost savings for the service company and an increased opportunity for dialogue with the consumer. Service providers that send out recurring notices, statements, or invoices for payment gain an interactive environment to create a dialogue with their customers.

For more information on online billing visit:
http://www.KCPL.com
http://www.cybercash.com/cybercash/billers

2.5 Is online shopping right for your company?

As covered in chapter one, online shopping is a process that provides your customers with the information they need to make a buying decision about your products or services.

- To create an effective e-commerce site, you must provide your online visitors with the information they need to understand your products and services.
- It is important to determine how much and what type of information you will need to provide to your customers.

Tell Me More

Online shopping provides your customers with the information they need to feel comfortable purchasing a product or service from your company using your online purchasing web service. Your web site must show more than your company's terms and conditions for purchasing a product. Most people have questions and need additional information from your company to feel confident making a buying decision. The information people need to make a purchase decision from your company depends on your product's sales process. Create an effective online shopping site, analyze your current sales, and create a logical flow in presenting this information online.

Some products are well-known to consumers before they enter a web site. Customers to those web sites are focused on price, availability, and quick access to the products. Other products are not yet known to visitors. People enter a site to learn more about the product. These products need to be supported by information and education so people can decide to buy.

Most consumers are shopping for low price and fast availability with brand name products. If a customer goes to an air reservation site to purchase an airline ticket, she will need little information other than the site's policies, and she will need access to an online program that shows flight schedules and costs. Most air ticket customers already understand what an airplane is, are familiar with the different airline carriers, and do not expect a ticketing office to provide them with directions to or from an airport.

A commodity site needs to provide convenient, fast access to tools so the visitor can gather the information she needs to make a decision.

Many products and services will need a web site that focuses on providing visitors to their site with the information to make a decision. If someone goes to Headroom to purchase a high-end headphone, he will have many technical and quality questions. Most likely he will be interested in the different classifications, features, and pros and cons of the different types of headphones. To sell headphones, Headroom needs to educate its visitors. Headroom has found that people want an outside opinion. To provide an outside opinion, Headroom has profiled customers who use their product. Headroom found that the most popular feature of its web site is a newsgroup it hosts. People can go to this newsgroup to ask questions, post comments, or read other peoples comments regarding headphones. Someone new to the Headroom site can go to the discussion site and read others' opinions and comments on Headroom products, getting an established consumer view.

Another company that has used online shopping to provide visitors to its site with a robust online shopping experience is Whistle Communications, found at www.whistle.com. Whistle sells integrated computer hardware and software solutions that connect a company to its Internet service provider, so the company can provide its employees with e-mail and Internet access (referred to as a POP server). Whistle has created an easy-to-navigate site that provides a logical flow to the product information people need. Since most people buying this type of computer solution are not yet familiar with the application, Whistle's navigation takes visitors to its site through the standard sales cycle questions potential customers have. Since Whistle is a relatively new company with a niche, noncommodity product, it needs to educate visitors on its product and provide backup information on who they are. Whistle has done this by including customer testimonials, customer case studies, industry awards, and press reviews.

Most companies that sell their products or services find that about 80 percent of the questions people ask are similar and that the answers to customers' requests have already been answered by someone within the company. By providing FAQs (Frequently

Asked Questions), supporting documentation, case studies, and testimonials, you can provide customers with the supporting information they need to make a buying decision. You may also find that your web site, with online shopping, can simplify your current sales process. When you provide your current customers with a location that answers their questions, they will not need to call a salesperson. This will lower your costs while increasing your sales staff productivity. Your salespeople can now focus on other accounts.

How to figure out what you should include on your online shopping site

Yes / No	Question	Response
	Is your product a commodity?	Yes—It is easy for people to understand the product. No—You will need to provide more detail defining and explaining your product's advantages.
	Are people familiar with your product even though they might not be familiar with your company?	Yes—It is easier to be credible when you are selling your product online. No—You need to establish your company's name along with your product. If your company's name is not known, you need to provide supporting documentation that shows you are credible.
	Do most people understand your product without an explanation?	Yes—They will need little online shopping. No—You will need to provide details for online shopping.
	Are people familiar with your company?	Yes—Use your company name to provide credibility. *(continued)*

Yes	Question	Response
No		
		No—Teach potential customers the benefit of your company by working with press, analysts, and existing customers to help build credibility.
	Does it take days or long conversations with a sales rep for a potential customer to make a decision to purchase your product?	Yes—Understand your sales cycle; know the questions people ask about your products. Create an online shopping site that highlights the choices people make to buy your product. Provide online shopping information to accelerate the sales cycle. No—Simple online shopping will help drive sales.
	Do you have a standard list of questions most customers ask?	Yes—Turn these into an FAQ list. No—Do research. There are standard questions you can identify and address.

2.6   How will your customers respond to your e-commerce services?

In order to anticipate potential customers' acceptance of your proposed e-commerce services, poll your existing and prospective customers to gain a better understanding of their access to and use of the Internet.

- For your online services to be a success, your customers need access to the Internet.
- It takes more than Internet access for a customer to buy on-

line. Buying online is a new way of buying; many people who shop online are still insecure about purchasing online.
- Even if your customer base does not appear to be ready for e-commerce, build your company's Internet presence to open new doors.

Tell Me More

Before creating an e-commerce site, ask your customers a few basic questions:

- Can they access and use a computer?
- Are they connected to the Internet?
- Have they visited a web site to get information on a product or service?
- Have they purchased a product over the Internet?

If the answer is a resounding "no," an e-commerce site will not be a productive addition to your business offerings. Don't assume you know the answers. To find the answer, you should do some basic research. Have your sales representatives ask their customers. Hire a research organization to conduct a study of your customers and market. Have them ask customers if they have an Internet connection and if they purchase online. Conduct this study every three to six months. You will be able to track the changes in your market. You may be surprised by the answers.

If you do business-to-business transactions, you might find that your customers have access to the Internet at home but not at work. Since the Internet is new, many companies are cautious, limiting employee access to the Internet. As the Internet grows, companies are understanding how to integrate business use on the Internet with employee responsibilities. Each year, a higher number of companies are providing their employees with access to the Internet. According to Dataquest, in 1996, few employees were accessing the Internet. By 1997, 20 percent of North American and some European employees had Internet access. By 1998, 50 percent of employees in North America and 20 percent of employees in Europe had Internet access. By the end of 1999, 78 percent of American employees and 70 percent of European employees will have Internet access.

Other impediments to success for e-commerce are your customers' comfort levels buying or ordering online. If your customers are connected to the Internet but don't feel comfortable buying online, it will take a while for you to receive a portion of your sales revenue from an e-commerce site. Even if your customers have access to the Internet, it still may take time for customers to purchase or order products online. You have spent years training your customers to purchase your products through your existing distribution channels. You will need to retrain your customers to use your online services.

E-commerce is new. Current or potential customers may feel uncomfortable buying online today, but they may start shopping online soon. In the future, customers who shop online will begin to buy online. By creating an online presence today, you can familiarize your customers with your online services, including online shopping and purchasing. If your customers are not shopping or buying from you online today, you should be monitoring them to see whether there is a shift to shopping or buying online. It is wise to stay on top of your customers when providing services. If you don't provide online services, your competitors will.

Your company's best defense is a good offense. By monitoring your customers and being proactive with web service, you can make sure that competitors don't undermine your business by providing new and different services online. Encyclopedia manufacturers did not see how technology advances were going to change their market. Encyclopedias like *Encyclopedia Britannica* and *World Book* did not see Microsoft as a competitor. Microsoft came out

Graph showing the growth of Intranet use

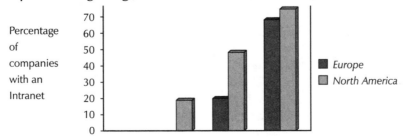

with *Encarta*, a CD-based encyclopedia. *Encarta* changed the way families provided research materials for their children and replaced existing paper encyclopedias. Likewise, Amazon.com has changed the nature of book buying. Companies like Walden Books and Barnes and Noble were not looking at the Internet for their next big competitor. By the time established booksellers created an online presence, Amazon.com had integrated its services into the fabric of the Internet. It's best for a company to be informed and prepared. If you wait for your competitor to prove the success of e-commerce services, it will be too late for you to enter the market and retain your share.

2.7 What are the basic elements of an online shopping service?

Online shopping supports the sales process by providing customers with the detailed information they need to make a decision.

- Companies can implement online shopping with or without implementing an online purchasing service.
- Online shopping will support the sales process and, in some cases, shorten the sales cycle.
- Your online shopping service needs to provide a description of the product, including pricing, delivery time and methods, and product warranties.
- More advanced elements of an online shopping service include descriptions and demonstrations of features, functions, and benefits of your product or service.
- An FAQ area provides visitors with an online resource to answer their questions.
- Competitive information provides potential customers with a method of comparing your products to other products. If possible, include or link articles that favorably highlight your product.
- Customer testimonials provide confirmation that others have similar issues and that your product fulfills their needs.
- Link to or provide related or additional information that

highlights your product, shows how to use it, or further completes your product desirability.

Tell Me More

You can implement online shopping with or without implementing an online purchasing service. Many companies start out by providing online shopping (product overview, answers to FAQs, and support) information on their web site. Depending on your company's ability to fulfill online purchasing requests, you may decide to only provide online shopping. By providing your customers with 24-hour-a-day, 7-day-a-week (24 × 7) access to information, you can support sales, in some cases shorten the sales cycle, and cut your administrative costs, since customers have access to information when they want it. Some people believe that potential customers are afraid to ask basic questions. Research has shown that from FAQs on an online shopping site, customers have a better idea of a company's product and feel more comfortable making the decision to buy.

The basic information that should be included on your online shopping service includes item description, price, product delivery methods, and return policy. Most people need this basic information to make a positive buying decision. Depending on the type of product or service you offer, you need to decide what other services you will provide to help people make an informed buying decision.

For products that are not obvious for most consumers, you will need to support the customer decision by including product features, the functions of those features, and a benefit to each feature. Bullet-point these lists to make them easier to read on screen. For products that are composed of many pieces, you may want to create an online configurator so customers can figure out what the solution will look like and cost. Dell Computers has found that the average customer visits its site ten times, reviewing product specifications and configuring systems, before purchasing online. If each online visit represented a phone call to Dell's support organization, and each support call cost Dell $5, the savings per sale would be $50. In a market where the per unit product price is falling well under $1,000 and product profit is 7 percent ($70), a $50 savings can drastically impact the bottom line and make the difference between profit and loss.

To support customers and to lower the number of direct questions to your sales organization, you should create a list of FAQs. For an existing product, your sales and support organization may have already compiled a list of customer questions. If not, it can provide you with the information necessary to create an FAQ. You should keep a list of the questions you receive from customers. If you continually see the same questions, you should periodically update your FAQ with these questions and the answers. Place the most frequently asked questions at the top of the FAQ. By placing common questions at the top, businesses have cut down the number of questions coming into the site by more than 50 percent, increasing customer support and lowering costs.

Visitors to your site may be encouraged to make a buying decision if they see how other people use your products and why they bought those products. Whistle, the company that provides Internet access equipment, includes success stories on its web site. It profiles a number of customers who use Whistle's product. It has found potential customers who come to this section of the web site can identify with the situation the profiled company faced and see how purchasing a Whistle's InterJet solved the problem. Case studies are a compelling tool for selling products that are complex, expensive, or have longer sales cycles. By developing feature functionality information and providing case studies with customer testimonials, visitors have the information they need to feel comfortable buying from your web site.

Competitive analysis can also highlight your product offerings. If you are selling ice cream machines, you probably have a feature/functionality comparison matrix of your ice cream machines to competitive models. Another way to help sales of your product is to provide an example of how people use it. Never assume people know as much about your product as you do, or that people know the best ways to use your product. By providing interesting examples of your product in action, you can provide potential customers with a reason for buying your product that will be beneficial for them. If you sell ice cream makers, you also want to have a section in your web site on award-winning homemade ice cream recipes as well as stories of people who have used your ice cream machine. You can include pictures of a party, the party's menu, and reasons the homemade ice cream topped off the event. You can include tips and techniques on making creamy ice cream, low-fat ice cream, or using fruit or mix-ins in an ice cream recipe. You can sponsor a contest in which people provide their favorite ice cream recipe. Make your site interactive by having your online audience vote for their favorite ice cream recipe. Providing additional information can increase the usefulness of your site to customers. Increasing customer use of your site in turn should increase add-on sales.

2.8   How will your distributors respond to e-commerce?

If you sell your products through distributors, you need to review your relationships and agreements carefully before launching the development of an e-commerce site.

- You may have a noncompete clause with your existing distributors that will preclude you from creating a consumer-oriented online purchasing service.
- It might be beneficial to create online purchasing services with your distributors.
- It's beneficial to support your distributors by creating an online shopping site that provides consumers with information on your product and points business to them.
- It is worthwhile to work with your partners, having them fill orders online.

Tell Me More

Most companies need to review their existing business relationships and contracts to study how changing their distribution patterns will alter their current relationships and sales channels. A candy company may want to sell its candy directly using its online purchasing service. Currently, the candy company distributes its products through regional distributors who place the company's candy in stores and candy shops. The candy company's distributor contract states that the candy manufacturer will not compete by selling directly to consumers. By selling online, the candy company will break its noncompete clause. Creating an online purchasing site is not always a technical and logistical decision.

A noncompete clause does not necessarily preclude creating an online shopping or purchasing service. The fastest growing area for e-commerce is business-to-business commerce. Instead of using your online purchasing site to target only consumers, it might be productive to target your partners.

To create an effective business-to-business e-commerce site, you need to study your current business practices. If distributors are faxing or calling in orders, it will be productive to build an online ordering system for them. An Extranet site provides e-commerce services within a password-protected portion of your company's web site. Partners can use this site to order products and to track shipments and legal information on the product.

You can create an online shopping service for end-use consumers. The service can build brand recognition, provide information about your products, and channel sales through your existing distribution channels. You can forward the consumer to one of your distributor's web sites or provide the phone numbers and addresses of the distributors in his area. The consumers can now complete their orders directly through one of your distributors.

It is probable that consumers are familiar with your brand name. When consumers are looking for a solution, they may be seeking you. You can use online shopping to support your partners by providing consumers with the information they need on your product. You can then electronically move the consumer to your distributor's retail or web site so he can purchase the product. This strategy will strengthen your brand in the industry, providing consumers with the information they need to make a buying decision, while supporting your business partners.

If you are a manufacturer, your shipping organization might be set up to handle large orders but not have the infrastructure in place to fulfill small, single orders. You might find that it is worthwhile to work with your existing distribution channel to fill orders generated from your online purchasing site. Your distributor should have an operation optimized to ship and support small single-product orders. Instead of reorganizing your shipping department to support single customer orders, you may strike a deal with your distributor where she can book single orders through your online purchasing site, funneling the fulfillment of these orders.

2.9   How can your online shopping site affect your business partners?

Before launching into an online shopping and purchasing site, it is necessary to understand the effect it will have on your business partners. Construct a site that will maximize the benefits of online access for both your company and your business partners.

- An online shopping site can shorten your business partners' sales processes.
- When you provide your distribution partners with online access to information, they can answer customers' questions more quickly, resulting in fewer errors, lower costs, and higher satisfaction.

Tell Me More

Creating an online shopping site can strengthen your company's relationships. Currently, you may send price lists and product guides to your distributors. Additionally, you may provide your distributors with standard business hour phone support. With an online shopping site, you can increase your accessibility by providing your distributors with 24 × 7 access to an online price list and product guide. An online product guide provides your distributors with a single location where they can find the latest information on all your products. With a paper price list, your distributors need to pick and choose components, hoping they have chosen correctly. With an online ordering system, you can design configuration guidelines to prompt partners through the ordering process, checking and confirming that the correct items are ordered.

With an online shopping service, you can create an interactive price list. The price list can be generated to show piece parts, whole configurations, retail prices, or your business partners' price. When a partner orders online, you can check his order and flag any orders that have missing pieces or questionable pieces. This can eventually save you and your business partners time and costly returns. With the addition of an FAQ and e-mail support, you provide your distributor with online access to noncritical questions. If the partner is located in a different time zone, or works in a retail environment where customers need support during nonstandard business hours, you can increase his support without changing the hours worked by your employees by providing him with the most recent product, configuration, and availability information online.

Online shopping provides your business partners with ready access to the information they need to do their job. Many business partners need access to more than product information. A building product supplier may need to procure special order products for building contractors. The building contractor needs to know when to expect delivery of his special order. A building product supplier will need to submit the special order to the manufacturer and receive pricing and product delivery information. If the manufacturer has created an e-commerce Extranet service, the supplier can access this service, order the product, and receive a delivery schedule and pricing. Later, when the supplier checks on the status of this order, he can return to the Extranet service to find the status of his special order. In the past, these types of transactions were typically faxed or called in. Since fax- and phone-based processes are dependent on human intervention, there is a lag time. If the building supply company is located in Hawaii and the manufacturer is located in New York, there is a six-hour time difference. Generally, there are only two hours in which the manufacturer's sales organization is available to take orders or provide the supplier with information. With a web presence, the supplier can provide 24 × 7 access to ordering and status information. When a supplier has online access to the information he needs, he can be more responsive by answering the customer's questions quickly. The manufacturer can provide better support and streamline operations, increasing his support without increasing support staff.

When you provide your distribution partners with online access to your information, your distributors will be able to answer their customers' questions more quickly, resulting in fewer errors, lower administrative costs, and higher satisfaction. Owens Corning (www.owenscorning.com) has a site oriented around home building products. The Owens Corning site has a great deal of information on its fiberglass insulation products, including the proper methods of using and installing them. A builder who needs details on fiberglass insulation to bid a project or submit plans to the local building department can access the Owens Corning web site and obtain the information she needs. By providing product information online, Owens Corning has shortened the sales cycle for its business partners. A contractor does not need to visit her local distributor to learn the insulation's R-value or to get information on measuring the job specifications to calculate the insulation needed. The Owens Corning web site provides the information a builder needs in order to make a decision. When a builder contacts her local building supply provider after visiting the Owens Corning web site, she has made a decision and knows what she wants to order. The building supply provider can focus on supplying the product. Owens Corning supports its distributors with sales leads by providing a "where to see/buy" section on its site. Visitors to its web site input their zip code and receive a listing of the stores located in their area. If the store has a web site, a hot link to the web site is provided.

2.10   What is online procurement and how does it work?

Online procurement connects a company's purchasing agents to preferred vendors as part of an electronic purchase procedure. A company's Intranet application is designed to guide the agent through the approval and fulfillment process.

- A new standard called OBI (Open Buying on the Internet) has been created to support business-to-business procurement.
- Online procurement streamlines the procurement process.
- This streamlining saves companies money by ensuring best-use practices for purchasing.
- The best-use practices, in turn, save vendors money by automating the order-entry process.
- Online procurement can be extended past office supplies to full corporate supply chain management.

Tell Me More

To assist the process of creating and integrating business-to-business electronic applications, a new standard has been defined, called OBI. OBI (www.openbuy.org) is a standard built around a common set of business requirements that supports technical architecture, specifications, and guidelines. The goal of OBI is to create a standard so companies can integrate their Intranet applications with different vendors' web-enabled applications. OBI makes it easy for companies to integrate their Intranet with many different vendors. With OBI, companies don't need to create different interfaces to connect to each of their vendors.

Online procurement integrates a company's Intranet, purchasing process, and preferred vendors into one online process. Here is how online procurement works:

1. An employee gets on the company's Intranet and accesses the corporate purchasing application. He can then view and choose the products he is interested in ordering. A company can include any kind of product an employee may be interested in purchasing (i.e., computers, office supplies, or machinery). When an employee chooses to view a product line, the company's Intranet automatically links the employee to the online shopping Extranet site of a preferred vendor. The employee sees the pricing and configurations available to his company on this site.
2. The employee chooses the model, quantity, and configuration he is interested in purchasing. The configuration and model information is transferred from the vendor's online shopping site to the employee's Intranet.
3. An application routes the employee's choice to the applicable chain of command for approval. Electronically, through digital signatures, the responsible people approve the purchase. If necessary, the purchase is routed to the purchasing department.
4. The approved purchase is then routed to the online purchasing site of the preferred vendor.
5. The preferred vendor sends the employee, with copies to all concerned, an e-mail confirmation receipt of the order and provides delivery information.

This kind of integrated procurement process saves time and money. Within a company, the paperwork necessary to procure products and the number of times the same information needs to be input into a system is diminished. Companies can increase the likelihood that an employee will use a preferred vendor, thus increasing their chances of meeting minimum purchasing quantities. This, in turn, increases the probability that the company can receive higher discounts.

On the vendor's side, paperwork is diminished, lowering the cost of doing business while increasing the likelihood that higher volumes can be reached. Currently, companies like Staples and Dell are providing additional discounts to companies that order electronically.

Supply chain management for office supplies using e-commerce is just the tip of the iceberg. Companies are looking at better ways to manage all expenses. Operating resources are 30 percent of the cost of running a business. Specifically, operating resources are nonproduction goods and services that businesses acquire and manage to run their day-to-day business operations. They include services, capital equipment, maintenance, repair, operating supplies, travel and entertainment, and myriad other items requiring approvals through internal business processes. Companies are looking at using e-commerce procurement to provide better tools to help them manage vendors and suppliers of all their operating resources. To stay ahead of the power curve, companies that provide operating resources need to see how they can enable their customers with e-commerce applications.

2.11   What tools can you develop to support customers, distributors, and partners?

You can increase the effectiveness of your online services by developing tools to support your partners.

- Include services that provide your partners with information on upcoming discounts, prices, availability, and/or warnings on a product.
- Integrate data-mining techniques into your partner Extranet

site. Data mining can be used to identify buying patterns and to create specials or incentives based on your customer's past buying habits.
• Integrate search engines, e-mail, and newsgroups into your web site to provide better services.

Tell Me More

When your customers, distributors, and business partners become familiar with your web site, they will learn that that is where they will find the most current information. They will view your site as the primary resource for such information. As more customers, distributors, and business partners use your web site, you will develop better ways to inform them. You will provide them with information on upcoming programs, or give them warnings on product changes. You can integrate **data-mining** techniques into your partner Extranet site. Data mining identifies buying patterns. You can create incentives to buy based on the ordering history of your customers, distributors, or business partners. Use these to increase sales and profits while simplifying your ordering process. Specialized services increase your potential solution since they provide customers, distributors, and business partners with important information while streamlining your sales process and giving incentives for them to make purchases.

If your company distributes to other companies that sell directly to the public, create a **marketing site** to support your distributors. On this site, you can inform your distributors about advertising programs you are running or about available comarketing programs. If your distributors use your graphics to create advertising campaigns (newspaper ads, fliers, mailers), create a location on your Intranet site where their advertising department has immediate access to your artwork, ensuring quality and accuracy in their ads.

There are many tools available to increase customer support over the web and to provide additional forms of support. Most companies integrate **e-mail** into their site. Integrating e-mail provides partners and customers with an easy way to ask questions. Companies like Sitebridge (www.sitebridge.com) provide programs that help web sites manage inbound and outbound e-mail.

Support trees and site search engines can assist partners by providing answers to questions. A support tree is a series of questions you ask your customer. Each question narrows the problem down to a more specific solution. If a customer has a problem with her car, an auto mechanic may ask her if she can turn the car on, if the lights turn on, or if she hears a funny noise. Each question narrows the scope of the problem and provides a path to an answer.

Site-based **search engines** are a convenient way to give visitors information. Search engines provide visitors with a utility to find what they're looking for. Most web servers come with a simple search engine. This simple search engine allows visitors to input a word or a string of words. The search engine finds any reference to a given word on that site. For more complex searches, a number of commercial search software programs are available. More sophisticated searches let visitors seek information by phrase, boolean, multiple keywords, or word context.

Newsgroups are another way of supporting customers. Your company can host a newsgroup to support customers' questions. A customer can post a question to a newsgroup. Posting a question is similar to sending an e-mail. The difference is that the question is sent to a newsgroup instead of to an e-mail address. Your customers can find current questions and answers by reviewing your newsgroup like an FAQ. Newsgroups can save your support organization from continually answering the same questions. To ensure that questions posted to a newsgroup are applicable, appropriate, and answered correctly, you should assign specific employees to monitor the newsgroup. Supporting customers via a newsgroup decreases the amount of time it takes for you to respond to customer questions while providing better service. You will also find loyal or experienced customers answering questions for you.

2.12 Will your company's infrastructure support the implementation and growth of e-commerce?

The creation and maintenance of online shopping and online purchasing services can defy traditional functional lines within an organization. Your sales, support, operations, and information services organizations are directly affected by your online services.

Before creating e-commerce services, you should identify the effect it is likely to have on each of these organizations.

- **Sales**—Orders can be processed directly by customers.
- **Customer support and Product service**—Due to online shopping, the nature of questions will change. So will the access method, since customers will be asking questions through e-mail.
- **Operations**—Traditional methods of ordering and fulfilling product orders will need to be integrated with new procedures developed to support online purchasing.
- **Information technology**—Web servers and web-enabled applications will need to be developed and supported.

Tell Me More

Online shopping and purchasing affects the workings of your sales, support, operations, and IS. In most organizations these functions work apart from each other. An effective e-commerce service is the intersection of these departments. It is necessary to understand the interconnectivity of these departments and to devise an e-commerce product team made up of members from each of these departments. Before initiating e-commerce services, look at each of these organizations to direct the effects of this new business focus.

Sales—Study the structure of your sales organization. What activities are the people in your sales organization performing? When your e-commerce site is activated, how will this change the sales department?

Companies that have instituted online shopping find that their sales cycle has shortened. They find that the number of customer calls has decreased and that their nature has changed. They also find that customers don't require brochures, specifications, and support sheets by mail since they can access this information from their web site.

This saves your company's call centers the time and overhead of answering calls and mailing or faxing the requests. The type and quantity of customer calls is also affected by e-commerce services. Without an online shopping site, your sales organization will receive most of the basic questions from customers. Your online shopping site will now answer most of these basic questions. Your sales organization will still be supporting customers who contact you over the phone, but an ever-increasing number of customers will be using your web services for answers.

Your salesforce will now be asked more difficult or customized questions. Typically these are the personalized questions customers ask if they need a specialized service. You will receive fewer questions from each customer, while your sales reps will have more time for handling account-management issues.

By integrating your online purchasing service with your business operations, you will find that the cost of fulfilling an order will decrease dramatically. Instead of a customer calling or faxing in an order, she will place her order on your online purchasing service. Online ordering saves you the expense of an order entry person to process the order. Since e-commerce is new, many companies are finding that many of their customers visit their online shopping service, but initially feel more comfortable buying the product by phone. Trends show that both online shopping and online purchasing will grow dramatically in the coming years.

Customer support and product service—Your online shopping service also affects your product support organization. Customers who shop and purchase online expect to be supported online. If you have an inbound telephone support organization, you will need to include support for incoming e-mail. Inbound e-mail in many ways is easier to support than inbound phone calls. Online customers expect a twenty-four-hour lag time between their e-mail question and an answer. Phone support organizations are targeted to answer a customer call within minutes. A twenty-four-hour lag between the time an online customer asks a question and expects an answer makes it easier for a phone-centric support organization to staff an e-mail response center. Besides e-mail support, many companies use newsgroups to support customers. Create a support newsgroup and have employees monitor the questions, providing answers or guidance as needed. Instantaneous answers to posted questions are not expected. This lag time provides your support organization with flexibility in staffing a support newsgroup.

To staff an online support center properly (e-mail and newsgroups), your support organization needs to identify employees who have good written communication skills. FAQs and support trees cut down on the number of questions that must be handled by a support organization. Your support organization is an excellent place to develop your FAQs and support tree since they already are familiar with the common questions your customers ask. By placing the most common questions at the top of an FAQ page, you can decrease the amount of calls you receive. It is interesting to note that company has a sixty-hour lag

CALVIN G. CHEW ○ Advisory Director

stion and provide a response. nel. To make this a successful promptly to e-mail questions sponsored newsgroups. Your that can provide a quick re-

Internet Shipping Group, LLC
9539 Enstone Circle ○ Spring, TX 77379 ○ 281.370.4191

fulfillment center becomes need to integrate the incoming order processing system. For the fulfillment organization, the origination of the order should be transparent (i.e., no difference between telephone and online orders). If you cannot integrate your e-commerce orders into your existing order entry process, create a secondary process whereby the e-commerce orders will be sent to your fulfillment organization.

The first steps in creating an e-commerce site are to revise your order entry, order processing, and order fulfillment processes. You must define where you can integrate online transactions into your existing process and create a parallel process. Take the time to identify the fulfillment process from the beginning. If you do not, you will receive online orders and have no set plan to fulfill those orders. Customers who do not receive products in a timely manner are not happy and will not recommend or use your service again.

Information technology (IT)—Critical to the success of your e-commerce site is the integration of e-commerce with existing computers and the identification of new processes and services. The cost and scope of this project is dependent on the size and scope of your e-commerce service and other services your company plans to integrate with your e-commerce service.

Your information technology department is most likely the organization that will be providing you with technical support, application integration, and application development. IS needs to be involved from the beginning to identify technologies and then integrate current and future systems.

2.13 Will your company change when you integrate e-commerce into your business direction?

Integrating e-commerce into your web site is a desired corporate direction, not just a technology decision. By providing e-commerce on the web, you make a profound decision to change the way your company will conduct business.

- When making this type of change, you should understand the effect it will have on your company.
- To obtain maximum advantage of this new business direction, you must thoroughly understand and integrate it into all aspects of your organization.
- Many areas of your company will be affected by this change.
- The departments most noticeably affected will be senior staff, sales, marketing, information services, support, accounting, and operations.

Tell Me More

When you change your business by creating an online distribution channel, it is important to understand the effect it will have on your company. To get the full impact of this new business direction, you will need to understand the effect of integrating web services into all aspects of your company. Many areas of your company will be affected by this change. The departments most noticeably impacted will be senior staff, sales, marketing, information services, support, accounting, and operations.

Senior staff needs to be educated to understand the importance of an online shopping and online purchasing site. The direction of your company needs to be integrated into the site. Don't confuse an internal corporate statement of direction with integrating your corporate message. Integrating internal messages and directions means executive incentives need to include integration of departmental web usage. Performance measures need to include integration of the web site into current business practices. Support needs to be prepared to answer the questions of your online customers in a timely fashion. The company's web address needs to be printed on all written materials including business cards, letterhead, brochures, and mailings. Likewise, senior management needs to incorporate these tools into their corporate messages.

You should educate your sales force on the benefits of e-commerce services to them and to their customers. E-commerce sites can bring new business to a company. Existing customers will also use the e-commerce site. An e-commerce site should be viewed by sales as a business service that assists the sales process and provides its customers with instant access to quality information. The customer benefits by having twenty-four-hour-a-day access to product information, support, and ordering. The salesperson benefits by providing her customers with better, more accurate service while being spared basic questions and administrative activities. For salespeople to incorporate the benefits of e-commerce into their activities, the company should build use of the site by bringing customers into the sales compensation program. For example, salespeople may get an award or a bonus for each customer who orders a product using the e-commerce site rather than by going through your company's traditional ordering process. This provides your salespeople with an incentive to move their customers to your e-commerce site.

Marketing is the organizational force driving an online shopping site. It will create the strategy and articulate the components of your site. Since the sales process, products, and market are constantly evolving, the components displayed on the online shopping site will need to be changed to reflect all market factors. The benefit of electronically publishing product information is that the lag time is short. Additionally, the web can be used by marketing to gather information on customers. Your company launches a product and provides information about that product on your online shopping service. Once the product is released, your company refines the marketing message based on feedback from sales and your customers. It is expensive to rewrite and reprint brochures to reflect this fine tuning. It is relatively easy to go onto your online shopping site and update the message with the new information. If your company tracks the flow of visitors through your web site and finds that particular product pages are of more interest to customers than other pages, it can make the popular pages easier to access, making the site more user friendly. Additionally, it is easy to update the online shopping site with customer success stories.

Your IS department will be involved in structuring, planning, and integrating web and e-commerce technologies into your online purchasing and shopping services; IS will integrate your web services with your current electronic systems. Your IS department should be involved from the earliest stages of an e-commerce site development project.

As discussed in article 2.12, an e-commerce site will change your support and operations organizations. Since support is typically tasked with answering customers' questions, the support organization will modify its current operations to respond to e-mail requests in a timely manner and to provide tools for customers to answer their own questions. Your operations department will integrate orders from your e-commerce site into your company's existing order fulfillment process or create a new order fulfillment process. Your IS department will naturally be involved with integrating these applications.

2.14 Chapter summary

To properly plan, integrate, and build effective e-commerce services, it is necessary to understand the effect e-commerce services will have on your business.

- Initially, you will need to identify the products and services you can potentially offer customers over the Internet.
- Before implementing an e-commerce site, you will need to identify the effect this site will have on your employees and your existing distribution channels.
- Create programs to educate employees and distributors on best-use practices of your e-commerce services.

- By taking the time up front to better understand the effect of new services, you will create better services and better communication. This should result in increased use, which should lower your costs while increasing your revenue.

Chapter 3

E-Commerce Technology

This chapter was developed to provide you with a fundamental understanding of the most pervasive technologies currently being used on e-commerce sites today.

Subjects covered in chapter 3

3.17   Putting it all together
3.18   Chapter summary

3.1   Do you have to become a programmer to create web documents?

The World Wide Web works well because it's based on simple universal technologies.

- HyperText Markup Language (HTML) is the simple computer language used to create documents that can be read from a web browser.
- An HTML document is made up of a series of codes that tell a web browser how to display a document.
- For those who want to create web pages but do not want to learn how to program in HTML, many word-processing programs can save a document as HTML.
- Web sites with many pages and interactive features should be created using site-oriented HTML editing programs such as Adobe Page Mill, MS FrontPage, IBM TopPage, or Claris HomePage.

Tell Me More

HTML, the universal language read by web browsers, is made of text with a set of special codes, or tags. These codes instruct a web browser on how to display the text document. Tags are a collection of instructions that define the various components on a web page. For example, to let the computer know where the title of the page is using HTML, the tag word "title" is placed before and after the words in the title.

If you have never written using a computer language, you are probably not interested in starting now. Luckily there are good software programs available called HTML editors. An HTML editor provides you with simple word-processing features that will turn your documents into HTML so you can display your information within a browser. If you are creating single pages of information, or you are responsible for updating a few pages on your web site, you can use current releases of products like Microsoft Word, Lotus Word Pro, and Corel WordPerfect. These are all word-processing packages that let you save the document in HTML. Many companies with large web sites deploy a decentralized method of creating web content. They provide a standardized template with the word processing software of choice. Employees responsible for developing web content are asked to use the template and save the document as HTML. When completed, the document is forwarded to a central web administrator.

The central web administrator may receive documents from many sources. After confirming that each document meets company standards for appearance, grammar, and spelling, the documents are inserted into the web site. Large web sites may have thousands of individual pages. It can become a nightmare to manually log, record, and link thousands of pages. Site-oriented HTML editors have been developed to help people responsible for managing large web sites. Site-oriented editing programs provide the same basic ability to create a document as in a word-processing package. You can create and define templates and include content. Good software packages have tools to help you build navigation, including graphics and basic templates. Additionally, these applications provide tools to manage sites such as automatically updating the navigation bars when pages are added or deleted, updating all pages when a template is modified, sitewide searching and replacement, hyperlink verification, and uploading only selected changes to your site. The most popular site-oriented HTML editors are Adobe PageMill, Macromedia Dreamweaver, SoftQuad HotMetal, Microsoft FrontPage, IBM TopPage, NetObjects Fusion, and Symantec Visual Page. These tools can be used to help you better manage your site.

For extremely large sites, databases are deployed to save and serve content. Sites like magazines and newspapers, where the content is constantly changing, use databases to store their articles. It is impossible to manually create a web site that can serve all the content found on a large news web site like CNN or CNBC. Instead, all articles are saved in HTML and stored as documents in a database. Visitors to the web site can input keywords and get a listing of articles that meet the search criteria.

3.2   How does HTML work?

HTML is a universal computer language allowing browsers residing on any type of computer to read a document. For those interested in learning more about HTML, here is a brief primer:

- To indicate how text should be displayed on a web page, the
  programmer surrounds the text with HTML tags.
- Some HTML tags, like the ones used to indicate a new paragraph, <P>, or a line break, <BR>, are stand-alone units.
- Every HTML document needs a title to describe the document's content.
- There are many resources for learning more about programming with HTML.
- The best way to begin learning about HTML is to plunge in
  and create your own web page.

Tell Me More

To indicate how text should be displayed on the web page, the
programmer surrounds the text with HTML tags. From your experience with a word-processing package, think of these tags as "re-
veal codes" that you need to create. HTML tags tell the browser
how to display or use the words. HTML tags are enclosed within
brackets. For example, the title for a document is created as follows:

<title>This Is The Title</title>

These tags are on/off switches. The first one says "begin title," and
then the title appears. The second tag tells the computer "end
title." The ending tags are the same as the beginning tags, except
they are preceded by a forward slash (/). A typical pair of tags
looks like this:

<B>and</B>

The tag <B> tells the program that the word "and" should be
displayed in bold type. In this example, the HTML programmer

needed to provide a begin and an end tag so the browser would know exactly what words should appear in bold.

Each tag pair is placed around the text or section that you want to define or mark up. If you want to begin a section of your document with a heading like "My First Web Page," you would use a heading indicator. There are six sizes of heading levels available in HTML. If you choose a heading size three, your HTML code would look like this:

<H3>My First Web Page</H3>

Some HTML tags are stand-alone units. This means that they can be placed by themselves in the middle of the text. The stand-alone commands are actions the program needs to perform so only one tag is required. For example:

<P> Begin new paragraph.

**
 Begin a new line or insert page break.**

Every HTML document needs a title to describe the document's content. The <Title> tag goes inside a section of the document called the header. The tag is not visible on the web page, but it is a very important element to every web document. The title should briefly describe the contents of the page, but it is not seen in the web browser's main section. The actual title is displayed on the top of the page, identifying it. This title is essential if you are going to register your page with Internet directories, since some directories use the title to categorize pages. Only one title per document is permitted, and the words between the tags should be in plain text. There shouldn't be any additional HTML tags or strange characters inside the title.

There are many sources for learning about programming with HTML. There is information on the Internet that will explain anything you could want to know about HTML. If you are interested in writing in HTML, you can use a search engine like Yahoo (www. yahoo.com) or Alta Vista (www.altavista.com) to find sites dedicated to writing in HTML. A good site to start with is Netscape

(Netscape. com), which has a good online HTML help section. Additionally, you can purchase a book on HTML.

A good way to begin learning about HTML is to create your own web page. All you need to start is a text editor like Notepad or BBEdit and web browser software. You should compose your HTML pages with your text editor and save them as text-only files with an .htm or .html extension. Then open the file in your browser to see what it looks like (keep in mind that an HTML document may look slightly different when displayed by different browsers). You can go back to the original HTML file as often as you like to edit it. The process is quite simple.

Here is an example of a simple page:

HTML	What it does:
<!DOCTYPE HTML PUBLIC "-//W3C//DTD HTML 3.2//EN">	Defines document as HTML
<HTML>	Beginning of document
<HEAD>	Start of heading
<TITLE>My first Web page</TITLE>	Title
</HEAD>	End of heading
<BODY>	Beginning of body
<CENTER><P><B><FONT SIZE = +4>MY FIRST <I>WEB</I>PAGE</FONT></B></P></CENTER>	Title centered with the word "WEB" italicized
<B>Some bold text followed by a line break</B>	Body of text
 	New line
<I>Some italic text</I>	Italicized text
<P>	New paragraph
<FONT COLOR="#000000">Link to </FONT>	Change text color
<A HREF="http://www.altavista.digital.com/"> AltaVista</A>	Link within text

<P>Another paragraph of things I can edit	More text
</BODY>	End of body
</HTML>	End of document

The above HTML produces the following screen:

MY FIRST *WEB* PAGE

Some bold text followed by a line break
Some italic text

Link to AltaVista

Another paragraph of things I can edit

Any time you visit a web page, you can see how it looks as raw HTML by selecting the appropriate command from your web browser's menu.

If you use Netscape Navigator 3.0, select the View menu, then Document Source or Frame Source. If you use Netscape Navigator 4.0, select the View menu, and then Page Source. If you use Internet Explorer 3.0 or 4.0, select Source from the View menu.

Links:
The Bare Bones Guide to HTML—http://werbach.com/barebones/
Composing good HTML—http://www.cs.cmu.edu/~tilt/cgh/cgh-new.html
HTML Teaching tools—http://www.hotwired.com/webmonkey/webmonkey/teachingtool/
HTML Primer—http://www.ncsa.uiuc.edu/General/Internet/WWW/HTMLPrimer.html

3.3   How do you design forms?

To provide customized pages or pages that visitors can use to input information, it is necessary to create a form.

- Forms provide an interface for visitors to give information, make requests, and choose or customize the information they receive. A web page that asks you to enter your name and address, use a pull down menu, or check a box to make a choice is a form.
- Features available for form design include text entry, radio buttons, check boxes, and action buttons.
- When designing forms, it is important to be sure you will obtain the information you require and that it will be easy for customers to fill out.

Tell Me More

Forms allow visitors to enter information, providing your web site with an interface for visitors to choose or customize the response they receive. HTML forms are similar to the paper forms we all

Different types of form fields

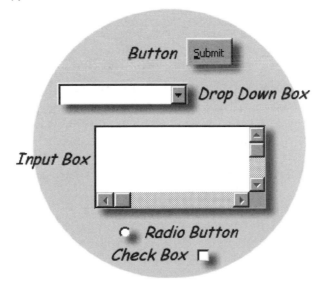

know. Information placed in an online form can be used for different purposes. It may be as simple as a form that gathers names, addresses, and e-mail addresses for an online mailing list, or it may be as complicated as an online configurator. You can create a form on your web site that allows a customer to preconfigure and price a product. Assume your company makes tables. You may have five tabletop styles, five leg styles, five types of wood, and five sizes. A customer may mix and match any of the above categories to create his own table configuration. Each of the four categories can be selected from a pull down menu. Visitors can choose any combination of styles by selecting the option they want in the pull down menu. Once they find the configuration they want to price, they can click the price button. On your server, you can create a program that will calculate the price for any combination of choices. The gateway program passes the customer's choices to the configuration program, then delivers the answer back to the customer.

Form fields provide different types of input fields that you or the designer use to create an online form. The different types of input fields include radio buttons, check boxes, drop-down list boxes, buttons, and input boxes.

Radio buttons—Radio buttons are a way of providing the visitor with a list or selection that lets them choose only one answer. If you have a questionnaire on your site, you may ask a visitor to select "male" or "female." With a radio button, they can only make one choice. If a customer is buying a product from your site, you may have features she will need to select before she can purchase the product. Your product may come in red, green, yellow, or blue. A radio button lets the customer select only one color.

Check boxes—Check boxes provide a visitor with a list or selection where he can choose any of the options on the list. If you are involved in the travel business, you can offer visitors a list of destinations and ask them to check all the destinations for which they want to receive information. You also can ask them what products they currently have; with a check box, they can choose multiple selections.

Drop-down list boxes—A drop-down or list box displays a list of predetermined choices from which the visitor may highlight and select one. Drop-down lists are a good feature when the list of options is very long and would take up a large part of the screen if one used a radio button. This feature is commonly used when visitors are asked in which state or country they live.

Buttons—Buttons are a graphics that can be clicked on to create a response. A button graphically allows your visitors to move from one page to another. A shopping cart graphic is commonly turned into a button. When visitors click on the shopping cart button, they are taken to an online purchasing site. Your logo can turn into a button. You can provide your business partners with your logo button for display on their sites. When visitors to their sites click on your logo button, they are transferred to your site.

Input boxes—Input boxes provide a space into which visitors type text. This enables you to ask a question and receive a specific answer or let the visitor ask a question. Input boxes are commonly found on online purchasing sites for customers to enter their name, address, and telephone number, or on a purchasing order, when you ask the customer for more detail.

Design a form on paper first. This helps you find what information you will need. If you are automating a paper form, use the paper form as the basis for the online form. Keep the layout simple and logical. People read top to bottom, left to right. Make sure your form follows this logical flow. Line up input box field descriptions and pull down box descriptions either over the input box, or on the left side of the page, with the input boxes aligned left. Line up check boxes and radio buttons to the left of the page, with the description to the right. Keep pages uncluttered; don't add graphics to your form unless they are needed to help the person fill it out. If you need specific information that the visitor supplies, you will need an input box. If there is a finite list from which the visitor can choose (e.g., state or country) you can use a pull down menu. If you are creating a support input form, you may decide that there are typically three types of support questions you handle. You may want to use a check box for each. If you have a predetermined number of products, each product may be listed in a pull down menu.

3.4   What is a gateway program?

The information that a visitor or customer inputs onto the screen
for your computer system passes to your server via a gateway program.

- The gateway program takes the information from the HTML
  form and interprets it for your server.
- The most popular gateway programs are CGI and ISAPI.

Tell Me More

Once the visitor completes the form and chooses "enter," the information in the form is sent to the server using a gateway program.
The server then processes the information based on how the application was designed. If you created the form to pass questions to
your support organization, the gateway program will pass the information from the form to your company's mail server so the support staff receives it via e-mail.

CGI—Common Gateway Interface is a task-oriented computer program that supplies a way to extend the capabilities of a
web server. A programmer uses a CGI program to take the information gathered from a form and pass it to a database or generate
e-mail.

ISAPI—Internet Server Application Programming Interface
performs the same tasks as CGI, but is much more powerful. ISAPI
is specific to Microsolf Windows NT. Microsoft's Active Server
Page uses ISAPI technology.

Gateway programs are the glue between web pages (forms)
and databases. There are software programs to facilitate this process, providing Generation four web developers with the tools to
create forms and integrate these forms with databases. These programs are designed with programmers in mind. The top interface
programs are Allaire Cold Fusion, Microsoft Visual Studio, Oracle
Developer, Silverstream, and Sun NetDynamics.

3.5   What is the role of databases in e-commerce?

Databases provide an electronic location to store information in a specific manner. This information can be accessed to make business decisions for your customers and business.

- A database may be as simple as a flat file, where information is stored in a table, or it may be a full relational database containing transaction integrity and millions of records of information.
- A web-based HTML form can be used to input or request information from a database.
- Integrating databases with web sites provides a company with a sophisticated way to send or collect information from visitors or customers.
- You can probably use your company's existing database(s) to support your web site.

Tell Me More

Most organizations are using some type of database to store and retrieve information. Databases are programs that electronically store information for retrieval. Your company might use a database to keep track of all your customers, your inventory, and your financial records. There are simple databases, such as flat files, or highly complex databases, called relational databases. The differences between flat file databases and the different relational databases are the number of records you can store, the size of the machine and operating system on which the database will run, and the sophistication of the available tools. Microsoft FoxPro is a flat file database while SQL Server and Oracle are relational databases. For small companies, where only one or two people need access to the data at a time, and the data is being accessed for standard uses like creating mailing lists or updating accounts receivable, flat file databases work well.

A relational database is a database that groups related subsets of data together for faster access. A sophisticated relational database will support millions of records residing on multiple computers and support simultaneous access by multiple users at once.

Relational databases deploy sophisticated controls so that different people can access the same data concurrently and the data does not become corrupted.

Companies can use forms as web-enabled interfaces to databases for users to add or access information from the database. If you have an online registration form where customers enter their names and addresses, you can create and integrate a database with this form. The database will be used to gather customer information. Once the customer information is in the database, it can be electronically accessed and manipulated. Many different types of sites can use this type of customer data entry form (e.g., an online auction site, a membership club, or a book club). You can use this type of form to provide your prospects and customers with information on product availability, pricing, shipping, product support, tips and techniques, and pertinent industry information. The customer fills out a form specifying e-mail address and information on which she wants to be updated by using either a pull down menu or a check box. You answer her request, and then store her information in a database. When you post new information or announce new products and services, you can create an e-mail that will go to all those in your database who asked to be updated on that subject.

The airline reservation system is a good example of a sophisticated, large database that is continually being accessed and updated by thousands of people at the same time. Sophisticated controls need to be implemented in the airline reservation system database so two airline reservation agents don't book the same seat at the same time for two different people.

The choice of database depends on the size, needs, and knowledge of your company. If your company is already using a database, you may want to extend its use to web-based applications. Most database manufacturers have created extensions, so you can web-enable your existing database's application. The most widely used databases are:

Oracle (www.oracle.com)
Sybase (www.sybase.com)
Informix (www.informix.com)
Microsoft SQL Server (www.microsoft.com/sql/)
FoxPro (www.microsoft.com/catalog/products/vsfoxp/)

3.6   What is data mining?

Data mining provides the tools that access information the company has gathered on customers and products.

- Data mining is a set of sophisticated tools provided by database companies that allow companies to access and analyze specific information found in large databases.
- Data mining should be used to automatically scan incoming information providing details for sophisticated analysis.
- Data mining can be used to customize your web site for your customers' and partners' convenience.

Tell Me More

Data mining is a series of computer tools that can be used to create sophisticated applications so companies can drill down into their database and find the information they need to make decisions and better serve their customers. All transaction information for a web site may be saved in a database. Marketing may be interested in knowing what geographic regions customers who are ordering certain products are from. Sales is interested in knowing the number of existing customers ordering from the online purchasing site and their activities. The same database holds answers to many different questions. Data mining provides valuable tools for gaining access to specific information.

Database companies provide tools that enable companies to analyze their activities. Information is gathered from a database using a query. Queries can be combined to help find complex relationships. From the data relationships, trends can be established. Automated data mining is a popular tool for companies that have large databases that consist of millions of records that need quick analysis or response.

Club cards have become a popular way retailers use data mining to manage their customer information, increase profits, and increase customer satisfaction. When a customer provides a store cashier with his club card, the store's computer instantly accesses the store's records for that customer. Data-mining techniques let the application quickly identify any buying patterns for both the product and the customer. The store can look for buying patterns and provide incentives to the customer, so he might make additional or complementary purchases.

A customer-buying pattern exists if a particular customer consistently purchases peanut butter. Grocery stores have found that most people who purchase peanut butter also purchase white bread. If on a particular trip the customer did not buy peanut butter, the grocery store may provide the customer with a coupon for peanut butter as an incentive. Providing an incentive to buy a complementary product is referred to as complementary selling. Online, this can be an interactive experience. Once a buying pattern is identified, the store provides the customer with discount coupons for associated products. This identification is done within seconds of the club card's being entered into the system. Grocery stores are the predominant users of club cards and data mining. They have found that they can increase their profit margin from a traditional 1.5 percent to more than 3 percent by using such targeted data-mining techniques, indicating that data mining is a cost-effective strategy.

3.7   How does encryption technology work?

As discussed in chapter one, encryption technology allows for secure transmission of data, including credit card information, over the Internet.

- Encryption scrambles characters into unreadable garble that is virtually impossible for anyone without a decryption key to unscramble.
- Public-key encryption is used in online purchasing sites to secure customer information and, most important, credit card numbers.

It's True: The "public" on public-key encryption refers to encryption that is publicly available.

Tell Me More

Encryption is used to scramble information sent over the Internet so that if it is intercepted, it is unusable. Encryption changes the characters into an unreadable code by moving the placement of the bits of data, thereby scrambling the message at the most basic level. The only way to retrieve the message is to have a key that can unscramble it. If the message were scrambled by moving the bits of data three characters to the right in the alphabet, the letter "T" would appear as the letter "W." The key will need to move each character back three places to the left so the data can be read. If the original message is:

This is the message

the encrypted message would look like this:

Wklv lv wkh phvvdjh

By just moving the letters three characters to the left, the sentence "This is the message" becomes unreadable. The encryption code for this example might be "3." It would be very easy to crack this simple code. Encryption creates complicated keys that are virtually impossible to crack, ensuring that transmission is safe from anyone who doesn't have the key.

Public-key encryption is a form of encryption in which the key is a mathematical formula. For example, it is easy to multiply 2 x 6. If someone asked you what numbers multiplied together gave you 12, you would have to guess (1 x 12, 2 x 6, 3 x 4, or 2 x 3 x 2). If the number were more than a thousand characters, the number of choices for multipliers would become so large that it would be impossible to guess. If you know the key, "2 x 6," the answer or encryption code "12" is very easy to figure out. Public-key encryption uses a large number and a multiplier to create the encryption code. This encryption creates a message that is very difficult to break, while only a small amount of data needs to be sent as a key to decrypt the message.

Public-key encryption support is built into most browsers. At the beginning of a public-key encryption session, the browser and the server exchange information about the cipher methods each understands. They then agree on a one-time key to be used for the current transmission. This makes it easy to use public-key encryption on your site since encryption is transparent to the user.

3.8   What are cookies?

Cookies are little reminders that a web site stores on a visitor's computer so that it can identify the visitor.

- Instead of continually asking the visitor for the same information, the program on the web site can save information to a cookie and, when it needs the information, read the cookie.
- The only information that a cookie stores is the information the visitor shares with the web site that created the cookie.

Tell Me More

Cookies are small files or tokens that are stored on a visitor's hard disk. They contain data about the visitor and the visitor's current session. Cookies are created so that an application on a web site can recall information about a current visitor's session. Without cookies, visitors will need to reenter their information on every screen, because the Internet is stateless: It has no ability to remember who a visitor is when the visitor goes from one page to the next.

Here's how a cookie might work. For an Extranet site, a cookie might store a customer's password. Each time he enters another page on the Extranet, the cookie authenticates him so he doesn't have to enter his password each time he wants to view a new page.

Some sites use a cookie to store the last page the visitor opened on that site. When the visitor comes back, the site can ask him if he wants to return to the page he visited last. The site then reads the location from the cookie and returns him to the correct page. This way the visitor does not need to bookmark or remember the location, which is convenient if you are taking a class online but need to go to a meeting in the middle of the class. Cookies are used within e-commerce services to support the online purchasing functions. For online shopping sites that include a shopping cart application, cookies store a unique reference number, so the server can track the visitor and save his transactions as he moves through the site.

A web site cannot read another company's cookie unless the other company provides it with a key explaining what the cookie means. The only information a cookie can save is that with which you provide the web site. A cookie does not know who a visitor is, unless he has filled in a form providing the web site with his name, address, and phone number. If a visitor fills in a form or buys a product on your web site, you can place a cookie on his computer identifying him. The cookie provides your computers with a customer number. You can use this cookie to customize the site for your customers. When a customer comes to your site, you can read his cookie, know who he is, and display information that is of interest to him. If he is an existing customer, you may display the status of his orders or you may display a selection of products you think he might be interested in based on his past buying habits.

3.9 What are the steps needed to create a secure online purchasing site?

There are five technologies that work together to create a secure environment for online purchasing:

Secure server—A server that hosts a web site that conducts secure sessions.

Digital authentication—A service that confirms that a secure server session is secure.

Encryption—A way of transferring information so no intruder can read it.

Merchant software—Software that is used to create an online purchasing service.

Electronic payment software—Software that is used to facilitate the payment of purchases on an online purchasing service.

3.10 What is a secure server and why do you need it?

A secure server is a computer that runs secure technologies, making it very difficult for intruders to gain access to confidential information sent over the Internet.

- Online purchasing applications should use a secure server. This safeguard ensures that credit card numbers can be sent over the Internet in a secure fashion.
- The technologies used on a secure server are:
  —Secure Socket Layer (SSL) Protocol
  —Secure HTTP (S-HTTP)

Tell Me More

It is important to deploy additional levels of security so hackers can't break into your communications lines and appropriate important business information like customers' credit card numbers. The first step in creating a secure environment for business transactions is to implement secure server technology.

A secure server is different from the computer that hosts your web site. It is a computer that hosts secure technology. It is used when you want to provide a customer with information or you want a customer to provide you with information and you want to ensure that no one else can gain access to it. Specifically, a secure server changes TCP/IP (Transmission Control Protocol/Internet Protocol), the communication underpinnings of the Internet, to make it harder for someone to break into an Internet transmission and steal the data being sent. The technology used on a secure server to make it difficult for intruders to intercept a transmission is called SSL or S-HTTP.

Secure socket layer (SSL)—We discussed in chapter one that the Internet runs on a protocol called TCP/IP. The protocol TCP/IP defines, to the computers on the network, what the information is and how it is being sent. SSL increases the capabilities of TCP/IP by adding a new layer on top of TCP/IP called the SSL Record Layer. When a customer enters a secure server managed by SSL, his browser makes a request to the server for a secure session. The secure server then opens up a special encrypted port for the online purchasing session. The data being sent is encrypted prior to being sent over TCP/IP. The SSL Record Layer manages this port to ensure that the session with the customer maintains its security. Additionally, SSL provides technology called SSL Handshake Protocol. SSL Handshake Protocol resides on the secure server and arranges for authentication and public-key encryption.

Secure HTTP (S-HTTP)—This technology from Enterprise Integration Technologies is a competing standard to SSL. Both SSL and S-HTTP create a secure port. Like SSL, S-HTTP supports both encryption and digital authentication. The difference lies in how and where these competing technologies create a secure port on a web server. Each creates the secure port at a different level of the communication session. SSL creates security using a network layer protocol whereas S-HTTP creates security using an application level protocol. With S-HTTP, a customer's browser requests a secure document from the S-HTTP server. The browser has a public key hidden in a secret place. It tells the server where to find its public key. The server then matches the browser with the key and confirms that the browser is authorized to access the secure document. The server encrypts the document and sends it to the browser. The browser uses its secret key to decrypt the message and display it to the user.

Deploying a secure server is relatively undetectable to your customers. They will not know they have moved from your site to a secure server site unless they look closely at their screen. They will then notice that the Netscape browser shows a blue line below the browser buttons and that the broken key in the bottom lefthand corner of their browser is no longer broken. If they are using a Microsoft browser, there will be a red line on the top of their browser and the open lock in the lower right-hand corner will be closed. Once the credit card information is supplied, your customers will automatically be taken to a page of their choosing on your web site.

3.11   What is digital authentication?

Digital authentication is a third-party service that validates that the web site receiving the information is the correct one.

- Digital authentication validates that the server receiving the information is actually a secure server and the correct one.
- To use digital authentication, you will need to register your site with a company that issues digital certificates, also referred to as digital ID.

Tell Me More

Digital authentication adds an additional level of security to a secure server. A secure server ensures that the transmission between the customer's browser and the server is secure. Digital authentication takes security to the next level and validates the server receiving the information as the correct one. That way, a clever thief can't spoof the network by rerouting server transmissions to his site in order to steal transactions.

When you design your e-commerce site, you will need to register it with a company that issues digital certificates. Digital certificates validate who you are and guarantee that your server is encrypting your customer's credit card information. The company providing the digital certificates provides your company with an encryption key that specifically identifies who you are and where your server is located. In other words, digital certificates are e-commerce inspectors making sure that the transaction is encrypted and the correct server is being accessed. Verisign is the best known company that issues digital certificates (www.verisign.com). If you are creating a secure server, you must register your company and secure server with Verisign in order to access their authentication services. Companies like Verisign require that their digital certificates be renewed annually.

As part of the digital certificate due-diligence process, a digital certificate company will do a background check on your company when you register. The digital certificate company checks to make sure you are in business and have a business license. Additionally, the digital certificate company checks to make sure your company has articles of incorporation, an address, and a phone number, and they will perform a Dunn and Bradstreet search on your company.

If your customers want to ensure that your site is legitimate, they can choose "view," then "document info" in their browser when they are on your secure server. Your digital certificate information will be displayed. If the digital certificate information does not match their secure site, they will know there is a problem and they will not complete the transaction.

For more information on digital authentication you can visit: www.verisign.com

3.12   How do you set up your web site to accept credit card transactions?

If your company had a storefront, customers could enter your business and hand you cash to buy a product. Online customers can't physically hand you cash or write you a check, necessitating that online purchasing sites create electronic forms of payment. The most popular are credit card–type services.

- Credit card payments work online similarly to the way they work in a retail environment.
- To do credit card transactions from your site, you need to support one of the online credit card payment processing services (Cybercash, PaymentNet, etc.).
- Additionally, you will need an Internet merchant account with a bank.

Tip: It will take a bank a while to process your request. Start working with a bank early in the process.

Tell Me More

If you were to open up a physical store, you would have to set policies on the types of payment systems you would accept. If you decided to accept credit cards or bank cards, you would need to set up a service with a bank in which your company had an account and the credit card transactions were verified and then deposited into that account. Online commerce is similar. Since an online customer can't give you cash or write a check, online commerce must use other methods of payment.

Credit card payments—The most popular payment system on the web for online purchasing is credit card payment. Since most consumers have at least two credit cards in their wallets, you are guaranteed payment, and you don't have to manage an accounts receivables process. Online credit cards are set up the same way as credit cards in a store.

Like a retail store, you will need to choose which credit cards you will accept. The most popular credit cards are Visa, Master-Card, American Express, Diner's Club, and Carte Blanche. Companies doing business in Japan should also use the Japanese BankCard (JBC).

To enable credit card transactions from your site, you need to contact one of the online credit card payment processing services (Cybercash, PaymentNet, etc.). These payment processing services provide you with software that resides on your secure server and connects you to their service. When a customer enters her credit card number on your site, your secure server accesses the payment processing service software. Since this access is initiated from a secure server, this transaction takes place over a secure line.

The payment processing service validates the credit card information so you can complete the transaction with your customer. You are then provided with a confirmation of the session. After the transaction takes places, the credit card processing service ensures that the money is placed in your bank account.

The following are the URLs for a few of the credit card transaction payment processing services:

www.paymentnet.com
www.cybercash.com

To accept credit cards on your web site, you will need an Internet merchant account with a bank (known in e-commerce language as an "acquirer"). Not all banks currently support Internet merchant accounts. Check with your bank and see whether it does or whether it is affiliated with a bank that supports Internet processing for business customers.

An Internet merchant account is designed to allow you to process Internet credit card transactions through a credit card processing network. Your bank will charge you to set up the account in addition to charging for processing each transaction. The charges will typically include the following:

- An application fee that ranges from $100–$400.
- A per-transaction fee (also known as the discount rate) that can range from 2 percent to 5 percent.
- Some banks charge an additional per-transaction flat fee from $0.10 to $0.30.

- Some banks charge a variable monthly minimum fee, which varies.

Obtaining a merchant account can take two to eight weeks; plan your process and your deadlines accordingly. Your bank will provide you with a Merchant Identification Number (MID) and a Terminal Identification Number (TID). You will need to provide your online credit authorization service with both of these numbers. The list of acquirers (banks) that currently support Internet credit card transactions include NPC and Sligos (Europe). Many banks that support traditional merchant credit card transactions also support online credit card transactions. A good place to start is with your bank.

3.13   Are there electronic payment systems other than credit cards?

There are many transactions for which credit cards are not optimal. Alternative payment services have been developed to support these types of transactions.

- Electronic cash micro-payments are used for transactions that are too small for credit cards (under $10).
- Electronic checks are used by use-based companies.
- E-mail can be used to authorize merchants or business partners to receive payments from a customer's account or to establish an account with a supplier.

Tell Me More

There are four basic kinds of online payment systems currently available: credit card, micro-payment, electronic checks, and e-mail based services. Not all transactions are optimal for credit cards. Additional payment services have been developed to support other kinds of transactions.

Electronic cash micro-payments—Small credit card payments, in the $.25 to $10 range, are not economical to process. Most people don't want to put small payments on their credit cards. Examples of where merchants will need small payments are:

- Pay-per-view areas
- Excerpts from content such as reports
- Small programs and utilities purchased online
- One-day passes to sites that otherwise require monthly subscriptions
- Pay-per-play games

Micro-payments are handled through electronic receipts. A consumer opens an account with an electronic receipt vendor. The micro-payment vendor provides the consumer with digital money in what is referred to as a digital wallet. A consumer can then purchase directly from sites that accept the same kind of electronic receipt payment. In a sense, the token works electronically the same way that cash works in nonelectronic commerce.

Before the micro-payment customer transfers the digital money to the vendor, it authenticates both the consumer and the vendor to make sure the money is going to the right place. An electronic cash vendor is CyberCash.

Companies that support micro-payments can be found at:

www.paymentnet.com
www.cybercash.com

Electronic checks—This is a service that allows clients direct electronic transfers from their bank to a merchant. Electronic checks are typically used to pay periodic bills. Utilities such as phone companies, electric companies, and water companies offer this payment method to improve collection rates, reduce costs, and make it easier for customers to take care of bills.

From the consumer's perspective, a customer first registers with the supplier, providing them with payment information (bank account number, etc.) and a preferred bill presentation. Depending on the services offered by the biller, consumers may be given a user name and a password for secured, authenticated access to the company's web site so they can view their balance online. The customers may alternately choose to receive their bill electronically, to have it mailed, or a combination of the two. For example, an e-mail notice that the bill has been posted on the utilities web site may be sent to a customer. When the customer accesses her bill over the Internet, she can view a full-color version of the statement—complete with graphics, logos, and full billing details. Provide your customers with the capabilities to customize the statement in ways that are meaningful to them (e.g., a telephone bill can be sorted by phone number, date, or length of call). After viewing the bill online, the customer may choose to pay the bill online with funds from her bank account. The payment process can be implemented through a service like CyberCash's PayNow secure electronic check service. Electronic checks appear on the consumer's monthly checking account statements in the same manner as debit card transactions.

You can build flexibility into your online payment options: If a phone bill isn't due on the day the consumer pays an online bill, the consumer can schedule to have the payment transaction take place at a later time. Once the consumer's payment authorization is received, the phone company submits an Electronic Funds Transfer (EFT) request to debit the consumer's checking account through the existing banking system.

E-mail-based services—First Virtual Holdings (www.first virtual.com) has an interactive e-mail messaging system that can conduct online transactions. Both the vendor and the consumer register with First Virtual. The customer registers her name, address, and telephone number over the Internet and then telephones First Virtual with her credit card information. A vendor registers online, then sends First Virtual its bank account information via postal mail. When a consumer purchases a product, she provides the vendor with her First Virtual PIN. First Virtual contacts the customer via e-mail to confirm the transaction. When First Virtual receives an e-mail approval from the customer, it executes the transaction, transferring money from the customer's credit card to the vendor's bank account. First Virtual provides an approval for the vendor to send the product to the customer.

3.14   What is a shopping cart and do you need one?

You either can build or buy software that is used for online purchasing. You can create your own software or purchase an off-the-shelf software solution. A few basic components are needed.

- A shopping cart is a link that takes a customer to a screen where he can choose the product he wants to purchase.
- Shopping carts use cookies to identify the list of products the customer has chosen to purchase.
- When the customer selects to purchase the items in his shopping cart, the transaction moves to the secure server.
- If your company has only a few products available, you can simplify the ordering procedure.

Tell Me More

The concept of merchant software is simple. Customers browse for merchandise on an online shopping site; when they see something of interest, they click on a shopping cart icon located on that screen. This action adds the item to a virtual shopping cart. At any time, the customer can choose to view his shopping cart's contents by clicking on a "view shopping cart" icon.

Shopping carts do not require secure transaction software. They are actually part of the online shopping site. There are two ways a company can set up a cookie. The first way is to have each shopping cart transaction stored in a cookie on the consumer's computer. The second way is to assign a customer ID and store this ID on a cookie. The customer's selection is stored on the merchant's server and accessed by the customer from the ID stored in his cookie. When the consumer asks to view his shopping cart, the information from the cookie is used to display the customer selection along with the selection's price.

The consumer can modify the information displayed on the order form at any time. When the consumer wants to purchase the items in his shopping cart, he can click a button that says "purchase." This action will move the session to a secure server. The shopping cart information will be transferred from the cookie to the secure server portion of the sequence.

If your company has fewer then ten products, it is not necessary to create a shopping cart application. It will be easier to create a simple order form. Order forms can reside on the secure server or on the online shopping site; it depends on the design of the site and on how much interactive description of the item is necessary. The order form consists of fields for quantity, product, and price. Off-the-shelf merchant software can include online order forms and shopping cart applications.

3.15   How does online purchasing work?

The online purchasing application resides on a secure server.

- After a customer chooses "purchase," she is taken from the shopping site to the secure server.
- The customer provides her mailing, shipping, and credit card information.
- The secure server verifies the credit card with a company like CyberCash. The transaction is then verified.
- Your bank receives the credit card funds from the customer's account. The customer's purchase transaction is placed in a database, ready for you to download to your processing center.

Tip: It has been found that if customers have to provide personal information before they choose a product, they will leave the online purchasing site at a higher rate than they would from a site where customers choose their products first.

Tell Me More

After the consumer decides she wants to purchase the product, she is moved to the secure server, where she fills in an information form providing her mailing and shipping information. This form then invokes software on the server to verify the electronic payment and approve the transaction. The customer receives a confirmation that the transaction was accepted, while the company receives a transfer of funds from the customer's credit card to its bank. It is recommended that the online purchasing site is set up in the following order:

1. Customer chooses product
2. Customer provides shipping address
3. Customer provides credit card information

After the customer completes the transaction, she is taken to a screen that tells her the transaction was a success. The information from the transaction should be used to generate confirmation e-mail, thanking the consumer for the purchase and providing her with pertinent information she will need to track the order. The transaction is placed in a database that can be accessed by the company's accounting system so it can be shipped.

3.16   What should you look for in a merchant software application?

There are many good merchant software packages on the market. Most companies need to choose which package to use.

- When looking at a software package, make sure it has the flexibility to support your needs.
- Companies who develop merchant solutions rather than going with an existing package typically have specialized needs that are not fully served by existing packages.
- Only a sophisticated information services (IS) organization should undertake this type of development work.

Tell Me More

There are many good merchant software packages on the market. Most companies need to choose which package they should use. To choose a package, it is important to understand your current and future needs. As we explained earlier, if you are selling fewer than ten items, you do not need to use a shopping cart application, since a simple order form will work. If you plan on growing your online product line to more than ten products in the foreseeable future, it is wise to go with a software package that includes shopping cart features, since upgrading will be time-consuming and create an added expense.

You need to look at your current accounting system. Most merchant packages save each of the transactions in what is referred to as a flat ASCII file. You will need to set up a procedure where you transfer the transactions to one of your computers for fulfillment. Before buying a product, ask for a record layout of the file where the transactions are stored. Provide this to your IS people. You will need to develop an application called a filter that lets your company's computers read the incoming file.

Check the software for flexibility. You will need to interface your online shopping site with the merchant software. The shopping cart icon on your online shopping page will take your customer to an order form in the merchant software for the product she selected. Merchant software products let you create a product list, for example, product name, price, tax, shipping fee, and details (color, size, etc.). Each product entered into the merchant software gets a code; you use this code in the shopping cart icon. Make sure the merchant software gives you the flexibility to integrate your web site with the software. If your customers are to provide details of their choices (color, size, etc.), make sure the merchant software makes it easy to do so.

The following is a list of features that you should look for in a merchant package:

1. Cross-platform support—The product runs on multiple platforms or on the platforms run by your company.
2. Foreign language support—If you are going to focus on an international market, you want support of translated versions of the display screens.
3. Unlimited simultaneous shoppers—How many shoppers and purchasers will you have on your site? Make sure the software scales to meet your needs.
4. Unlimited product support—If you have, or someday plan on having, a large catalog of products, you want a package that will support your entire catalog and has the flexibility to provide subgrouping of items.

5. Online help—If customers have questions, you may want an integrated pull down help menu.

6. Payment information encryption—You will want to support encryption and standard payment services.

7. E-mail notification of orders—Automatically have order reports sent to people in your company via e-mail. The system lists the total orders for that day, week, or month for the people on them. (Tip: Don't choose notification of each order; it will make your life miserable.)

8. Automatic shipping—This provides you with the flexibility to choose the shipping company and system (i.e., flat fee, by weight, or by location).

9. Group shipping—If there are three products being shipped, will the system make you add the shipping cost of all three products, or can you create a group shipping table?

10. Automatic tax calculation—Customers input their zip code or country and the merchant system should be able to calculate and display the tax.

11. Personalize the order system—The ordering system should allow for easy customization and modification of the ordering pages. The page creation tool should work with popular HTML editors like PageMill or FrontPage. Global edits (search and replace) should also be supported.

12. Statistics—All kinds of information is being gathered when people enter your online purchasing site. Make sure your package is flexible in the way it provides you with statistics like sales, traffic, and consumer information. The reports they show may look great, but does the package let you easily modify existing reports to meet your needs?

13. Database and spreadsheet upload—This feature gives you the ability to create a spreadsheet or database on your computer and then have the package upload and support it within the merchant server.

14. Order database access—This feature allows for accessing orders securely through the SSL server. The package should be configured to e-mail you daily site information (number of orders, total revenue, etc.). The actual orders

should not be sent via e-mail, but should be sent or viewed securely, using the SSL server.

15. Credit card authorization—Authorization provides you with support of electronic payment systems.

16. Associates tracking—Associate programs let you provide partners with a specific URL to your online purchasing site. Any transaction that comes through this URL gets a discount, based on an arrangement with the partner. You can also arrange commissions for any sales generated from that URL to the partner.

17. Site search—Is there a built-in search engine?

18. Interface to other applications—This feature hooks to database applications like Oracle, Informix, Microsoft SQL, and IBM (IMF, DB2).

19. Discount calculation—The discounts are based on order level or customer information.

For a listing of merchant storefront software you can visit on the Internet go to:

http://www.Cybercash.com/tp_list/kat.html

3.17 Putting it all together

This chapter provides you with an understanding of the different technologies to create an online shopping and online purchasing service. To ensure you understand what this chapter has provided, read the "Tell Me More" section for:

• Technology and steps that customers are exposed when shopping and purchasing online
• A look behind the scenes (what is really going on)
• An overview of the technologies you need to implement popular features

Tell Me More

There are many pieces of technology needed to create an online shopping site. To ensure you have a perspective on the flow of events from a customer point of view, here are the steps through which a customer goes to purchase a product on an e-commerce site.

Putting it all together from a consumer's point of view

1. A customer enters your online shopping site, choosing products she wants to purchase by clicking on a shopping cart button.

2. At any point, she can view her shopping cart by clicking on a "view shopping cart" button. Within the shopping cart, she can delete items or change the quantity and characteristics (color, size, etc.) of the items she is purchasing.

3. When she wants to purchase the items in her shopping cart, she chooses the "purchase" button. Then, she is transferred to a secure server with the contents of her shopping cart.

4. The customer is provided with an itemized list of her shopping cart for approval; she chooses "accept," thereby placing a firm order.

5. A screen appears that asks her for her name, address, shipping preference, and credit card information. She fills in the screen and chooses the "accept" button. She is then moved to a screen that tells her that her transaction was accepted. An e-mail is sent to her confirming the billing address, items ordered, and date she should expect to receive the product.

Many of the technology steps in creating an easy and secure environment for online purchasing are not seen by your customer. Here is the behind-the-scenes flow of actualizing an online transaction.

Putting it all together from a vendor's point of view

1. Visitors enter an online shopping site. They view the products. A shopping cart icon is included on each product page. When the consumer sees a product he likes, he can click on the shopping cart icon. The item number is then stored in a cookie on the consumer's computer. At any point, the consumer can view the contents of the in-basket. A CGI script takes the information from the

cookie and uses it to generate a page displaying the items the customer has chosen. The visitor can then add to or delete from his shopping cart. When the visitor is ready to purchase the items in his shopping cart, he clicks the "purchase" button.

2. The customer is then taken to a secure server. Behind the scenes, a digital certificate verifies that the secure server is secure and that the merchant and consumer are who they claim to be. The items in the shopping cart are displayed for approval. The consumer clicks on "approve."

3. The consumer is taken to a new form where he is asked to fill in his name, address, and credit card information. The consumer then enters his personal information into a form and his electronic payment information is encrypted and sent to a payment processing service. His credit card information is verified and approved. The transaction is then completed.

4. The consumer is transferred to a "thank you" screen.

5. Payment is moved from the customer's credit card account to the business' bank.

6. Some of the information from the transaction is used to fill in a confirmation e-mail that is automatically sent to the customer.

7. The transaction information is placed in a database.

8. The merchant company periodically (hourly, daily, etc.) transfers this information to their order entry system.

Technology Matrix

The matrix below provides you with an overview of the types of pages that are typically implemented on a web site and the associated technologies needed for that type of page. Each choice for a web page may require that a different type of technology be implemented.

Table 3.17   Typical Web Technology

Choice	Technology
Simple online shopping service including FAQs and text-based product overviews	HTML

Extranet	Password protection through HTML
Site customization, product configuration	Gateway program to access database
Mailing lists	Gateway program to access database
Online purchasing	Secure server, encryption, merchant software, integration with existing applications

As the matrix above shows, the decisions you make on what type of site you are interested in implementing directly affects the technology you will need to use for your implementation. Most FAQs, feature functionality reports, and product overviews are text with a few pictures. Text is created as HTML. Many companies use a design firm to create a template for their HTML pages. You can ask your design firm to integrate the templates it develops for you into the HTML publishing package you decide to use. Like a word-processing package, when working with an HTML publishing package, you can choose a template before you create a document. When you create the document, the template formatting and design elements (i.e., layout, bullets, fonts, and spacing) are automatically used.

A designated person within your company can use the HTML publishing package with the integrated templates to create and update text portions of your site. If you want to create a form that lets the visitor customize the information he receives from your site, you will need to hire a programmer to write a program that lets you integrate a form with a database that then generates an HTML page. Creating interactive features will provide your visitors with a more personalized service but will also take longer and cost more to develop.

3.18 Chapter summary

To create e-commerce services you will need to deploy several different types of technologies. Whereas the technologist needs to understand how to implement the technologies, it is important for the business manager to understand what the technologies are and how they can be used so that they can better communicate direction.

- The basis for any site is HTML. HTML provides the text and structure to a web site.
- Forms are the visual interface from a web site into a company.
- Gateways are the bridges between a form and technologies within a company.
- Databases are the workhorse of the Internet, providing companies with a method of categorizing and managing information.
- E-commerce applications are developed from HTML, forms, and databases.

Chapter 4

Creating E-Commerce Services

This chapter provides you with strategies to successfully implement an online shopping and online purchasing service.

Subjects covered in chapter 4

4.1   How should you define your e-commerce goals?

Before creating an online service, it is important to know your company's goal(s).

- Creating a clearly defined goal provides direction to the process of creating effective e-commerce services.
- Goals should establish expectations.

Tell Me More

Before creating an e-commerce service, it is best to clearly define your goals. Many companies create goals that are not measurable or specific. It is difficult for a company to create and stand behind a new and effective product without a specific goal. Examples of business objectives that should not be used when creating an e-commerce service are:

- Having a presence on the Internet
- Increasing awareness
- Improving sales
- Reducing costs
- Increasing number of hits
- Getting more repeat visitors
- Increasing length of time users are on the site

Business objectives are specific; they include hard measures like server-use statistics (who did what and when, sales figures, and items sold and conditions). Surveys and interviews are soft measures that can provide you with good business objectives. You can use inferred results based on server statistics, such as user impression studies, user opinion surveys, and interviews.

Examples of effective goals for an e-commerce service are:

- Reducing support center costs by 30 percent over the next twenty-four months.
- Receiving 25 percent of corporate revenue through e-commerce within the next four years.

- Decreasing sales and support costs by 25 percent over the next four years by moving to online applications.
- Increasing awareness of your products among employees by 25 percent by the end of the third quarter.
- Extending the organization online to increase sales and customer retention by 25 percent.
- Reducing the cost of customer support by 15 percent by leveraging online communications technologies and maintaining excellent service.

Decide your goals for creating an e-commerce service. Make sure they are clear and provide specific enumerated targets.

Links: The twenty reasons to put your business on the Internet: http://www.net101.com/reasons.html

4.2   How do you develop an ROI for your e-commerce services?

Most companies demand a defined ROI (return on investment) to be created when a new product or service is being proposed. There are three basic types of ROIs for web services:

- Cost chain—tells how this service saves money
- Value chain—increases service to increase sales or provide additional value
- Transaction chain—reduces a process to save money

Tell Me More

Calculating your ROI for a web site is not necessarily linear based on the content and services you are providing. You may have to create multiple analyses to actually figure out the ROI. The most common ROI used is a **cost chain.** A cost chain replaces a current manual process with an automated process. You save money and time by automating a process. Your online shopping site might house some of your brochures. If before you established an online shopping service, your marketing department mailed out sixty brochures a month, with an online shopping site it might only mail out ten brochures a month. If your costs are $5 per brochure and $5 for mailing, totaling $10 per brochure mailed, total cost per month saved by providing brochures on your online shopping site is $5,000. The one-year cost chain ROI for online data sheets is $60,000.

Value chains increase current services. You build an ROI on a value chain by giving a dollar amount to the cost of acquiring and retaining a new customer, or upselling or cross selling an existing customer. It is more difficult to create an ROI for a value chain than for a cost chain, since you need to place a dollar amount on existing nontangible service. You may already know that your average cost for acquiring a new customer is $10,000. Your goal may be to use your web site to expand your customer base. You may decide that your goal is to generate one hundred new customers over the next two years from your web site. Your ROI for acquiring new customers will be $1,000,000.

Transaction chains typically eliminate a process. Transaction chains are made up of a collection of cost chains. The savings come in cutting time, effort, and people. A transaction chain ROI can be used for your online purchasing site. Let's say you currently have a four-step process for product ordering: 1) customer contacts order entry, 2) order entry faxes order form, 3) customer faxes filled in order form, 4) order entry inputs order into system. Perhaps this process takes place over three days and uses one hour of employee time. With online ordering, the process takes five minutes and uses none of your people. If your people handle forty transactions a week, you save yourself forty man-hours a week or one person. And since the product is ordered three days earlier, you can provide faster turnaround. The average fully burdened cost per employee per year in the United States is $180,000, which you may have saved with this transaction chain.

Most information on your site will fall into one of three categories. You can identify the ROI analysis to use based on the category of your new services.

1. **Real-time information**—This information often consists of static information like product descriptions and features, press releases, and corporate information. A web site replaces fax and

paper distributions. Using the Internet to distribute information increases a company's opportunity to create and update information. It lends itself to a cost chain ROI analysis.

2. **Transactions, commerce, and tools**—Frequently changing, real-time, and interactive information can be linked to existing computer systems. It is used for store locators, order status, online purchasing, and inventory management. It lends itself to a transaction chain ROI analysis.

3. **Relationship and value exchange**—Promotional, personalized, or targeted information is usually tied to external marketing programs, mass customization, banner advertisement, and comarketing programs. It lends itself to a value chain ROI analysis.

4.3   What market segment should you be targeting?

The first step in getting started with the creation of an online shopping and purchasing site is to identify the market segment on which you are going to focus.

- Create a list that identifies all the services you can provide on your web site that will help you reach your goals.
- List all the possible market segments that your site can support.
- Choose one market segment and create the online services needed to support that site.
- When the first market segment's services are complete and functional, focus on the next market segment. Identify what services can be used for that segment and what additional services you will need to create.

Tip: Companies that go after too many market segments at once create services that are probably not focused on any one market. Their sites usually do not meet targeted goals.

Tell Me More

To help you decide the appropriate content for your e-commerce services, you must decide what you want to accomplish on your online shopping site. Earlier we discussed how to create an effective goal for a site. Use the goal you set as the basis for this exercise.

List all the possible ways you can accomplish your goal.

If your goal was to "extend the organization online to increase sales and customer retention by 25 percent," you might create a list that includes:

1. Providing tools so customers can track their orders
2. Working with the sales department to find the ten most frequently asked questions (FAQs) and providing a list with answers
3. Providing up-to-date sales materials
4. For a company with a large product catalog, providing a search tool so customers can find products easily
5. Providing an online news report highlighting subjects that are of interest to your customers
6. Providing online ordering

Other possible topics that might be included in this exercise are:

1. Online training
2. Consumer shopping
3. Distributor shopping
4. Product information
5. Access to corporate presentations
6. Sales success stories
7. Branding information
8. Product support
9. Online purchasing
10. Customer tracking
11. Order tracking
12. News bulletins
13. Sample/file downloads
14. Volume discount management
15. Government regulations

List all the possible market segments for your site.

A goal that increases sales or increases support can involve multiple markets. You might sell directly to the public, you might sell through retailers, and you might sell to other manufacturers. List all the possible markets you can focus on in your site. After identifying your objectives, organize the activities based on the markets they will serve.

Possible markets

1. New consumers
2. Distributors
3. Partners
4. Existing customers
5. Retailers
6. Other manufacturers

It is difficult to create a site that supports multiple markets from the start. It is easiest to choose one market to pursue at one time and create a successful site for that market. Once you build a site that serves this particular market's needs and your company reaches a predefined target, you can move to supporting the next market. You may decide to work with your distribution partners first. To support distribution partners, you should place basic product information on your Internet web site. Most items on the list of services to support distributors are well-suited for an Extranet site. Develop an Extranet site that includes online shopping, online order tracking, online order placement, and marketing tools including product definitions and pictures, product copy, and sales presentations. Create a marketing campaign to make your distributors aware of your Extranet site. You use your sales force and order administration people to help with this awareness campaign. When 25 percent of your orders are received online, you will move to your next target market.

You may decide that your next target market is consumers. You can use the existing infrastructure of product information, order tracking, and order placement with this new market. You can decide that you will need to modify your online purchasing site so you can fulfill consumer orders directly. Once your online purchasing site is complete, run a marketing program focused on consumer awareness.

It is advisable to go after one market at a time. It is easier to manage costs when taking this focused market approach, since you only need to develop the tools used by the market you are targeting. As you grow your markets, you can reuse tools, incrementally developing new tools when they are needed. Keeping your site targeted keeps your organization focused and provides employees with the time and knowledge to better focus the site on the market being addressed.

4.4 Do you need to complete your site before you begin publishing it?

After you select the tools needed to create a successful service, you might find that some tools take longer to create than others. Online purchasing usually takes longer to create than online shopping.

- Plan both the shopping and purchasing services at the same time.
- It is easiest to build and publish your online shopping site first.
- With your online shopping service available, you can monitor the flow of people on your site, refocusing navigation where necessary.
- You can use an 800 number on your site to fill online orders while you are building your online purchasing site.

Tip: Create a new 800 number, which makes it easier to track orders that are coming from your web site.

Tell Me More

Once you have decided on your target market, you will need to decide where to start. Plan both the shopping and the purchasing site together.

It is easiest to build and publish your online shopping site before you implement an online purchasing site. You can begin to provide information to your target market as soon as possible, giving it an opportunity to move to online services. Most companies find that it takes much more time to integrate online purchasing with their existing systems than to build an online shopping service. Most of the materials you will need to develop your online shopping site already exist and are relatively simple to reconfigure for the Internet. Because most online shopping sites consist of simple HTML documents, you should complete your online shopping site first.

If you publish your online shopping site before your online purchasing site is available, you won't have a way to fulfill orders online. You can provide an online order form that customers can print out and fax back or you can have your customers call an 800 number to purchase your product. An 800 number just for online shopping customers provides you with an easy way to track the leads your web site is generating. Even after you install your online purchasing site, it is worthwhile to have a separate 800 number for online customers, because some people will not yet be comfortable with ordering online. Before you have your online purchasing site available, you can provide a screen telling online customers that your purchasing site is under construction. By providing a date when the online purchasing component will be available, you can begin marketing to those customers who like to purchase online.

There are many benefits to publishing your online shopping site while you are developing your online purchasing site. You can provide timely information to customers sooner. You can use this time to better direct your online shopping site. You can monitor visitors' progress through your site, identifying what pages they land on and where they go. You can then use this information to make changes to your site's flow. To make it easier for visitors to find popular pages, they should have direct access from a navigation bar. Another popular tool you can provide visitors is an e-mail address by which they can contact you directly. You can use e-mails sent from your web site to identify common questions and add these questions to your FAQ. You might find that common questions e-mailed to you are already on your FAQ and have their own web page. By receiving e-mails on questions already answered, visitors to your site are telling you they are not reading your FAQ or getting to the web page that provides them with the information. Check to see how many pages the visitor needs to view to reach the page of information or the FAQ. Identify whether the page is clearly labeled on your navigation bar. You might reduce the number of e-mail questions by simplifying your navigation or better labeling much-used web pages. Publishing an online shopping site while you are developing your online purchasing site makes it easier and more productive to add one later.

4.5   How should you structure the content on your site so that it closes business?

The goal of any e-commerce site is to generate and close business. Salespeople understand that there are distinct phases of the customer buying process. You need to think about that all-important customer buying process when you are designing your site. The key is to provide the information your customers need to move through each phase of the process so they arrive at the decision to make a purchase. Phases of the buying process are:

- Need identification
- Research
- Product selection
- Product purchase
- Buyer's remorse

Tell Me More

The objective of your site is to generate interest, answer customer questions, and close business. Experienced salespeople will tell you there are distinct phases in the customer decision process. During each of these phases, your customer's questions and needs will be different. Your site's success will be enhanced if you provide potential customers with the information they need to move through each phase of their decision process. If you already have an established product sales process, your salespeople can probably inform you of the behaviors and questions they see in each of the different phases. The following five phases are typical to most customers:

The first phase is **Need identification**—A real or apparent need triggers or inspires someone to be interested in a product or service. For example, someone may identify a problem and need a solution. Alternatively the interest may be sparked by:

- A salesperson demonstrating a new product or service
- A conversation with a neighbor or a coworker
- Exposure to an item on a TV show or news program
- An interesting article in a paper or a journal
- An advertisement

Your site can alert a potential customer to her needs by identifying her issues. Then, it should show how your product can fill those needs. If you are selling a training class on Internet basics, you can provide examples of issues that similar companies have had, for example: "A manufacturing company has implemented an Intranet and placed web browser software on employees' desktops. The company now needs a training tool its employees can access to learn how to use the web effectively." A manufacturer that has recently introduced web browsers to its employees will relate to this example and read on about your product.

Research—Once a consumer has identified a need, she will need to research alternative solutions. The process may be as simple as reading a label on a new product seen at the grocery store or as complex as hiring a firm to research the issues and perform an analysis. Your online shopping site should provide good basic information on your product or industry (including problems solved, testimonials, etc.). Anyone researching her need should be able to find the information she needs for further definition on your site. If your site answers a person's questions completely and clearly, that person has little reason to go elsewhere for her information. If you provide customers with the information and utilities they need to do this research, you will increase the likelihood that they will choose your product. This is a critical step in capturing visitors and turning them into customers.

Product selection—After a potential customer researches and defines her needs, she analyzes the possible alternatives including features, benefits, and costs of different solutions. You may include competitive analyses, cost-benefit tradeoffs, customer testimonials, and case studies on your site showing how others have solved the same need with your product.

Product purchase—Once the customer decides to buy a particular solution, she will obtain the product from the most convenient source.

Buyer's remorse—After people purchase a product, they may fear that they have made a bad decision. Buyer's remorse happens regardless of the size of the purchase. Most cancellations and returns occur because of buyer's remorse. Any actions or information your company can take or provide to ensure the customer he has made a good decision will help to keep the sale. Customer testimonials, positive articles on your company or product, positive comparisons to other products, and cost-benefit analyses of your product or service are features of your site that can help people feel that they have made the right decision.

Each one of these buying phases should be addressed in your online shopping service. When a potential customer lands on your site, you should clearly highlight the needs he has, how your products fulfill these needs, and the benefits he will derive from your products. Once he decides that your product will solve his problem, your online purchasing site should provide an easy and convenient experience.

Link: What makes great content—http://webreference.com/greatsite.html

4.6   What should you include on your online shopping site?

After you decide who your initial target market is, you will need to display all the activities needed to create successful online shopping.

- Decide on the type of information the visitor will need.
- Decide whether this information should be placed on your Internet site or Extranet site.

- Identify who will be responsible for developing the material and monitoring it.
- Identify what technologies will be needed to create that activity.

Tell Me More

After you decide on your target market for your online shopping site, you should display all the activities needed to make it successful.

In order to achieve your goal, decide on the types of information a visitor to your site will seek. Earlier in this chapter, you listed different online services you should develop to reach your goal. Use this list as the basis of the matrix in the following exercise. Create a complete list focused on all market segments. By listing all the services for all target markets, you will see what information overlaps. This information may be added. Add columns to help you identify what will most benefit your completed e-commerce services.

Table 401 is an example of an online shopping development matrix. Our sample site's goal is for the company "to obtain 25 percent of the sales over the Internet within the next twelve months." The company has two market segments: direct consumers and distributors. The company has decided to serve its distributor channel first. Some activities on the web site will be used for both markets; others will need to be modified for the second, direct customer market.

The table has two versions of customer stories. One of the customer stories is focused on Internet consumers and named customer testimonials. Customer testimonials provide prospects to the online shopping site with information on why others made their purchases. Customer stories are also being developed for the distributor Extranet site; they are called "customer sales case studies." This document is a private view examining why the customer bought the product. The distributor version will include the same information provided in the customer testimonial, along with additional sales examples and information that distributors can use to increase their sales. Since the distributor version includes the customer version, it is easier and less expensive to create both case studies at once. By initially outlining all the documents you plan to create as a result of all the planned phases of an online shopping site, it is easier to spot what items overlap and what technologies can be reused, saving time and money in the long run.

The following explains each of the fields within Table 4.1

- Content—Web pages that need to be developed.

- Department—What department is responsible for creating the web page.

- Release Date—Target date the site will be activated with content.

- Type of page—The type of template you will need.

- Layout—The design firm lays out the page with the data provided by the member of the department responsible for content. The design firm inserts approved graphics.

- Template—Provide an HTML-based template. In the future, employees can use this template to create and update text-based web site pages.

- Outline—Your marketing department provides an online tutorial (using an online training product).

- Acrobat—An Adobe acrobat file (portable document) is created from the provided graphics document.

- PP—A Power Point presentation is created and saved as HTML; an FTP version of the Power Point presentation is provided so distributors can download the presentation.

- Form/DB—A database-enabled program is written. Visitors see a form interface screen. Based on their selection, a database is queried and the appropriate information is displayed on the visitor's screen.

- Priority—Importance of that information to the site.

- Frequency of Updates—How often will the information be changed?

Table 4.1   Content for an Online Shopping Site

Content	Department	Release Date	Type of Page	Priority	Frequency of Updates	Market
Internet (customer site)						
Data sheet	MarCom	June 1	Acrobat	High	Low	Both
Brochure	MarCom	April 1	Acrobat	High	Low	Both
Product advantages (benefits)	Marketing	April 1	Template	High	Low	Both
Product overview	Marketing	April 1	Template	High	Low	Both
Product specifications	Marketing	April 1	Template	High	Low	Both
Learning tutorial	Marketing	Nov 1	Outline	High	Low	Customer
Where to buy	Sales	Nov 1	Template	High	High	Customer
Pricing	Marketing	April 1	Template	High	High	Both
Upgrades	Marketing	April 1	Template	High	Low	Both
Support (FAQ)	Support	May 1	Template	High	High	Both
Business showcase (testimonials)	MarCom/ PR	May 1	Layout	Med	Low	Both
Subscription registration	Marketing	Nov 1	Form/DB	High	Low	Customer
Latest release information	Marketing	Nov 1	Template	Med	Med	Customer
Extranet (distributor site)						
Technical presentation	Marketing	Mar 1	PP	High	Low	Distributor
Sales presentation	Marketing	June 1	PP	High	Low	Distributor
Future release information	Marketing	June 1	Template	Med	Med	Distributor
Configuration guide	Marketing	May 1	Form/DB	High	Med	Distributor
Directory of distributor resources	Sales	June 1	Template	High	Med	Distributor

Content	Department	Release Date	Type of Page	Priority	Fre-quency of Updates	Market
Distributor development funds	Sales	June 1	Template	High	Med	Distributor
Customer/sales case studies	MarCom/ sales	May 1	Layout	Med	Med	Distributor
Competitive database	Marketing	May 1	Form/DB	High	High	Distributor
Pricing page	Marketing	Mar 1	Template	High	High	Distributor

- High—information changes weekly
- Med—information changes monthly
- Low—information rarely changes

4.7 How do you design a site to support people with varying needs?

To create a successful site, you will need to design your site for people with varying needs.

- Some people know what they want and are annoyed if they need to page through product information before ordering.
- Other people need to access information in order to make a decision.
- By creating a product-listing page, you can support both types of visitors on your site, providing each easy access to the services they want.

Tell Me More

Once you have created a site with straightforward navigation, you will need to develop an online shopping site that provides people with information in a way that is easy for them to access.

Customers who have already made a decision to buy dislike

paging through volumes of supporting information and long product descriptions. The trick is to provide detailed information for customers who want it, while enabling customers who are not interested to bypass the details.

Sales and customer satisfaction levels have been increased at most of the successful sites that list all available products on an overview page. When the customer first enters the product section of your web site, you can display a bare-bones list. If at this point the customer knows exactly what he wants, he can click on the purchase button next to the product name. If the customer needs to see more information on this or other products, he can click on the name or description to be taken to that product's online shopping site.

The overview page lists each product, with one short sentence describing each item, its price, a link to more information, and a shopping cart button or a link to the online purchasing site. Product pictures are only included if they are small thumbnail graphics. Larger pictures would slow down the product-listing page. Your goal is to serve pages as quickly as possible so people can move through your site to get to the information they want.

Many products need more than a one-sentence description. If someone knows what he wants, a short description provides him with a quick way to ensure that he is choosing the correct product for his shopping cart. A purchasing agent tasked with ordering parts will know what he wants to order by the product's numbers and will not want to page through supporting detail. A designer might need to read the detailed specifications and see a picture of many products so he can be sure he has ordered the correct part. An effective site caters to both types of customers.

Link:
12 Web Page Design Decisions Your Business or Organization Will Need to Make:
http://www.wilsonweb.com/articles/12design.htm

4.8   What if you want to tie your online purchasing site to internal applications?

By connecting an online purchasing site to internal databases, you can integrate your e-commerce site with your company's normal operations.

- The simplest and most secure method of transferring information from your online purchasing site to your internal applications is through a batch transaction.
- Some companies tightly integrate their online purchasing site with their established internal operations, providing customers with instant access to inventory availability and order scheduling.
- The more tightly your online purchasing site is integrated with your internal operations, the harder it will be to create and the more security you will need.

Tip: Before launching your online purchasing site, test it out by shipping products to friends located within the area you are supporting.

Tell Me More

The simplest and most secure way to integrate your online purchasing site to your existing applications is to create a batch entry process. This is when you set up a procedure whereby you move all the transactions on a daily basis from your online purchasing site to your corporate systems. Your existing accounting system reacts to these new orders as if someone had keyed the online transactions through your order-processing system. If you are not using a merchant software package from the same software company that created your accounting system, you will need to integrate your online ordering system with your accounting system. To do this, you will need to create a simple filter. The filter will make sure the information from your online purchasing system looks like the data in your accounting system. Once this simple filter is created, it is easy to integrate online orders with orders from other sources. Since batch transactions are saved and posted, orders are not interactive, and customers do not get immediate feedback on product shipments and inventory availability. Back orders and ship dates will have to be provided to customers in a separate e-mail after you have posted the transaction to your accounting system.

Some companies choose a more integrated online purchasing application—one they can integrate with their existing accounting applications and inventory databases. This integration provides customers with instantaneous online verification. Online customers can be informed immediately if the merchandise ordered is available for shipping. Integrating online purchasing directly with your existing accounting applications requires sophisticated programming and security. You should not underestimate the amount of work or the cost of interactively tying your online purchasing site to your existing applications. This level of integration can provide your customers with excellent services.

To integrate internal applications to any Internet application, you need to create sophisticated security procedures. Since the Internet is not a secure environment, it is recommended that you create a series of firewalls (hardware and software security) between your internal accounting applications and your online purchasing applications. There are a number of databases that hold important company information that will need to be accessed for interactive applications. Some of the corporate databases that may be accessed or updated from an online purchasing site are inventory, accounting, and fulfillment (shipping). It is important to make sure intruders cannot access internal systems when the information is transmitted between your online purchasing site and your company.

4.9   How do you create an internal infrastructure to support e-commerce?

It takes time and coordination to develop procedures to integrate your internal infrastructure with online purchasing. Companies need to modify their internal procedures and processes in order to expedite products purchased from their online site.

- Existing computer systems need to be checked to see whether they can process transactions coming from the on-line purchasing site.
- Accounting needs to integrate and monitor transaction revenue from the online purchasing site.
- Your service organization will need to answer and access records created from the online purchasing site in order to support customers' questions.
- Your inventory control department needs to monitor inventory levels for sales of online products.
- Your shipping department needs to be staffed and ready to send out new orders, giving shipping options and costs.

Tell Me More

The most difficult aspect of integrating e-commerce within a company is filling online orders. You will need to evaluate your existing infrastructure and test whether this infrastructure can meet your e-commerce needs. You will need to create procedures and, in some cases, create work teams to support the fulfillment of your online purchasing orders.

If your company manufactures consumer products and sells these products through distribution channels, and you have solved any channel conflict problems by selling directly, you may want to sell your product through the Internet. Your internal infrastructure may not be set up to receive and ship single orders. Evaluate your back office accounting system and check whether it can accept single orders and process them. Specifically, you will need to review the inventory and shipping module of your accounting program to see whether it supports single-item shipments. If your current system does not support single-order transactions, you will need to upgrade or purchase an accounting system for online purchasing order fulfillment.

Orders received from your online purchasing site will need to be given different identities so your accounting department can easily monitor which distribution channel sent an order. You may be using your online purchasing site to support multiple distribution channels (e.g., customers, distributors, retailers, and partners). You want to identify which channels generate an order so you can track the effectiveness of your site. A direct way of doing this is by creating a unique transaction number based on how the customer entered the online purchasing site. Consumers will get transaction numbers starting with six, while distributors' transaction numbers will start with seven, making it easy for your accounting organization to run reports identifying who is ordering from your site.

Once the transaction enters your site, other departments can access this information. Your customer support organization will need access to customer orders so it can support customer questions and returns.

You may need to identify a separate area within your shipping facility to store your e-commerce inventory. This area will need to be more closely monitored for stock levels since e-commerce customers expect orders to be shipped within a day or two. Your accounting software will need a way to print bills and shipping receipts, and shipping staff will need to pick, pack, and ship products in a timely manner.

4.10   How do you create an e-commerce fulfillment policy?

Part of developing an e-commerce site is creating and communicating policies:

- Online flow detailing what will happen when customers purchase the product
- E-mail invoice confirmation after they purchase a product

Tell Me More

Many Internet novices think that once they enter a secure server, they have no choice but to purchase the product. You should clearly state that a transaction can be canceled at any time before the visitor clicks on the "purchase" button on your online purchasing site.

Online purchasing flowchart—A simple flowchart detailing what will happen when visitors enter your secure server will alleviate many of their concerns. An example of a purchasing process description is:

An e-mail sent to a customer after she purchased a product online

---

Subject: Order Number 123-456
Date: March 23, 2001 14:31:12
From: Order Processing <orders@upandaway.com>
Organization: Up and Away Baloon Rides
To: you@yourcompany.com

Thank you for purchasing a baloon ride from Up and Away Baloons. Your oders number is 123-456. To check on your order or get more information on your baloon ride you can visit our web site or call 800-123-4567.

Ordered by: You
Address: 123 Main St. Anytown USA
Transactlo number: 123-456
Qty: 1 baloon ride for 4 people
Dates of use: March 23, 2001 - March 23, 2002

---

1. Choose the product and press "purchase."
2. This will automatically take you to our secure server where the purchase will be carried out.
3. Fill out the customer information form on the secure server.
4. Enter your credit card number.
5. Click on the "purchase" button to purchase the product (this executes your purchase).
6. You will get a screen with a listing of the transaction, telling you the transaction was successful. You will also receive an e-mail invoice.
7. Your selection will be shipped to you in three to six working days. Once your product is shipped, you will receive a second e-mail providing you with a shipping tracing number.
8. You can change your mind at any point in the purchase cycle before step five.

After your customer purchases a product or service from you, she should be taken to a click-through screen. A click-through screen is a screen that displays information and needs to be clicked on to move the customer to another screen. The click-through screen should thank your customer for her business, telling her the transaction was a success and providing her with a summary of the transaction.

Confirmation e-mail—You should automatically send your customer an e-mail confirming her purchase, detailing the products she has ordered and the price she has paid, listing the expected shipment date, and providing a hyperlink to a support web page on your web site.

Some useful items on the confirmation e-mail receipt include:

1. Date
2. Time
3. Name of person ordering the product
4. Ship-to address
5. Transaction number
6. Quantity and product ordered in clear language (don't use internal abbreviations)
7. Price paid including tax, shipping, and handling
8. A hyperlink web page the person can access if she has any questions
9. Expected shipment/arrival date (e.g., product will be shipped within three working days)
10. Return and cancellation policy
11. A sentence asking the person to review the transaction to make sure all the information is correct

Once your customer has completed her online purchasing transaction, you will need to decide where in your site you want to send her. You can place your customer back on your web site's home page, on your product home page, or on a page with add-on specials. You need to direct your customer to an appropriate location, since you want to retain customers after transactions are made. Ask your salespeople what questions customers have after they purchase a product. Navigate online customers to a page that addresses those types of questions. If your customers experience buyer's remorse, navigate them to a page of customer testimonials.

Alternatively, if customers are looking for add-ons to your product, navigate them to a product page detailing add-ons.

4.11 How do you update current fulfillment policies for the web?

Many companies that conduct business traditionally will need to review their current policies and identify where these policies need to be modified for business over the web. Policies that may need to be modified are:

- Shipping policies
- Return policies
- Support policies

Tell Me More

When you are creating your e-commerce service, you will need to evaluate your current policies and ensure that they apply to e-commerce.

Shipping policy—You will need to evaluate your shipping policies and procedures. For example, you may decide to store transactions on your online purchasing server and daily batch-transfer your orders to your accounting system. You then can process and ship orders. If you accept the batch of orders from the online purchasing site at 12:00 PM, you can inform customers that any order received before 11:45 AM will be shipped out that day. You can staff your shipping department to process orders in the afternoon. Another shipping procedure will be method of shipment. Many companies include two forms of shipment: overnight and ground. To simplify the procedure, some companies charge a flat rate for both. For example, it might cost $15 to overnight a product to Dallas and $20 to overnight a product to Miami. You can charge a flat $20 for all overnight shipments.

Before releasing your online purchasing site to customers, you should test whether it works as projected. It is a good idea to ship trial orders to several destinations scattered throughout the area you geographically support, using all shipping methods you plan to offer. Ship the product to friends or family and check when the product arrives. This gives you a realistic estimate of how long it takes to get the product from your location to your customer.

If your shipping application is not integrated with your online purchasing site, you should e-mail shipping information to your customers. When the product is shipped from your company, the customer record will be updated with the shipping tracking number. You can have an e-mail generated automatically and sent to customers after products are shipped. The e-mail will thank the customer for his business and provide him with the tracking number for his order. Within the e-mail, you should include a URL to a web page located on your web site. This web page can provide customers with information such as a link to the shipper for order tracking, tips on using the product, and ways to contact your support organization.

Return policy—You will need to evaluate your return policy for e-commerce transactions. It might take a product ten days to get to a customer. You might decide to give customers a twenty-day window from date of shipment to request permission to return the product. You can then provide a thirty-day window in which products can be physically returned. You should clearly state all your return policies on your web site and in all e-mails. Since most products bought over the Internet are paid for by credit card, you will need to work with your acquirer (bank) to create a credit card return process. After you receive a returned product, your bank can credit the customer's account with the price of the product.

Support policy—You will need to develop customer support. If you currently support customers, you may decide to funnel e-commerce customers into your current support operation. You should provide your support center with access to e-commerce customer records.

Some companies selling products through retail channels do not support customers on their web site. When they start selling products directly to consumers, they need to make a distinction between customers who bought via e-commerce and customers who bought through retail channels. This allows for a separate support site for e-commerce customers. The URL for this site is only given out in the e-mail sent to customers after they purchase the product. The e-commerce support web page(s) provides shipping, return, and support policies along with phone numbers and the e-mail address.

4.12   What should you know about selling internationally?

The Internet provides companies market reach outside their traditional geographical boundaries. The issue is selling and supporting goods and services internationally.

- Shipping goods internationally
- Selling services internationally

Tell Me More

When creating an e-commerce site, companies need to decide how they want to service and support international markets. An e-commerce site will provide your company with customers worldwide.

  You need to decide if your company can support international sales. International sales issues are different for services than for products. It is costly to ship products from the United States to international destinations. Shipping costs alone may be higher than the price of the product. You will need to find a person in your company who is well-versed in international trade. This person will create the necessary information and paperwork to ship the products abroad. For companies that see a large international market, this might be an opportunity to work with a distributor located in the new markets you are targeting. You can sell your products internationally by sending them to an international distribution company. The international distributor will ship your orders to customers located in their agreed-upon region. This approach eliminates your need for an export department. Since prices are displayed on a web page, most companies that sell to consumers and distribute their products internationally roll the international distribution costs into the customer's shipping costs. For example, if it costs $10 to ship the product from the local distributor to the customer, and the per unit cost for the company to ship and stage the product to the distributor is $15, the company will charge the customer $25 for shipping.

If you decide that your company does not have the resources or sales volume for international shipments, you should clearly state on your online shopping and online purchasing sites what geographic areas you support.

For service-based companies, staging is not an issue. You will need to identify whether your service is legal in other countries. You should contact your local State Department offices to make sure there are no legal barriers to selling your services in an international market.

For more information on exporting internationally, visit the U.S. Government's Small Business Administrations export site (*http://export.2rad.net/*). This site has comprehensive information on issues facing most businesses that are planning on exporting products and services.

4.13   Chapter summary

Creating a clearly articulated business plan is a necessary step in creating an effective e-commerce site.

- The basis of any business plan is definable goals, a projected ROI and identification of the market you will be targeting.
- Your plan can be used to identify resources, content, and technology needed to create the services necessary to reach your goals.
- You will need to identify your customers' buying patterns to better design services focused on their differing needs.
- Your internal infrastructure—including systems, policies, and procedures—will need to be reviewed to see how you can integrate new online services with existing services.

Chapter 5

Hosting and Supporting E-Commerce

This chapter provides you with guidelines and recommendations for creating, hosting, and managing an e-commerce site.

Subjects covered in chapter 5

5.1   Where should you host your online purchasing site?

You will need to implement a secure server for your online purchasing site. The secure server may be located at the same location as the computer that hosts your web site, or it may reside in a completely different location. Common choices for hosting online purchasing sites are:

- ISP hosting—You choose an Internet service provider to host your online purchasing site.
- Internal hosting—Your IS organization runs your online purchasing site.
- Turnkey solution providers—Depending on your industry, there are companies that can host an online purchasing site, manage your inbound 800 number calls, and do your product fulfillment.

Tell Me More

Your online shopping site and your online purchasing site will not reside on the same computer. As we discussed in chapter three, an online purchasing site resides on a separate, secure server. Over the Internet, you can transparently and easily link people from your online shopping site to your online purchasing site. Only people that understand how online purchasing works will know that they are not purchasing from the same computer that they were visiting for online shopping. The Internet's support of seamless links gives you the ability to choose where you want to host your online purchasing site. Your choice depends on your business considerations. The three main choices for online purchasing hosting are ISP, internal, and turnkey.

   ISP—Many ISPs can support their customers' e-commerce services. When hosting your e-commerce site with an ISP, you will use the computers located in the ISP's facility and create your site using the merchant software the ISP runs. Some ISPs provide customers with access to a secure server to run their own applications. Use an ISP if you do not have a sophisticated IS department to run Internet-based applications, are unsure how many transactions you will be getting from online purchasing, or need to access a standard merchant application.

Internal—Some companies need to host their online purchasing site internally for strategic and directional reasons. Before you decide to host a secure server internally, examine whether you have, or are willing to allocate, the resources and expertise to manage a secure server. The most obvious reason for hosting a secure server internally is control. When you host internally, your company's IS organization manages the server. If you host your site internally, you have control over what software will run on your server. This gives you the flexibility to run off-the-shelf and internally developed, or off-the-shelf but customized software.

Companies use internally developed packages when they have specific needs, such as very large or complicated applications. Developing merchant software is not easy. Merchant software is complex. Creating it should only be undertaken by companies that have experience in developing software and have a large IS budget.

Financial institutions provide customers with access to financial or transactional records. Most financial institutions must have complete control over access to their customers and account data. Hence, they need to control their own servers.

Host your system internally if you have a very dynamic, highly sophisticated site like Amazon.com's, Microsoft's, Dell's, or Cisco's. Since your revenue depends on your e-commerce services and your site may be changing hourly, it might be difficult to find an ISP set up to support a site as large, dynamic, or volatile as your mission-critical merchant applications.

Turnkey—A new group of companies is emerging to support e-commerce. We call them turnkey providers. Many turnkey providers are call centers and fulfillment houses. Since they are already working with their clients to support inbound telesales activities and to ship products, it is natural for them to offer e-commerce support. A call center that supports your sales can help you design and support your online purchasing site. If they do not have the resources to create a customized experience for your visitors, you will have little flexibility on the site they provide.

Table 5.1 can help provide you with information on finding

the best solution. As you can see, hosting a site internally gives you the greatest flexibility, but it also costs the most in equipment, people, and phone lines. ISP hosting is the most popular solution since you can use the ISP's resources, experience, and computers, but if you have unique or specialized needs, it might be difficult to find an ISP that suits your needs. A turnkey solution is the simplest, the least flexible, and the easiest to implement, though you will be charged for the ease and simplicity.

5.2   How do you select an ISP to host your site?

There are many benefits to hosting your site with an ISP, but it is important to choose an appropriate one. The following list shows what is needed to decide with which ISP to work:

- Software support
- Hardware support
- Network resources to support your goals
- Experience
- Technical staff

Tell Me More

Many companies host their online purchasing site with an ISP because ISP's have the experience and scalability to support e-commerce sites. A good ISP has already installed and managed e-commerce software and has an existing relationship with the different vendors.

A good ISP has the resources to expand with your business. Most ISPs charge you by the number of transactions on your site. If your site starts with ten transactions in week one and moves to 100,000 transactions in week five, the ISP has the resources (hardware, software, communication lines, and people) to quickly and transparently move your application to a more robust system (scalability). Avoid a site that is slow to process, or worse, an online purchasing service that is inaccessible.

1. *Software support*—Most ISPs have specific merchant-server software applications that they support. When you choose an ISP,

Table 5.1 What Type of Site Do You Need?

Your Needs	Internal Hosting	ISP Hosting	Turnkey Solution
You can use off-the-shelf software packages.	Yes	Yes	Yes
You want to use internally developed software.	Yes	Maybe	No
You want to use a combination of internally developed and packaged solutions.	Yes	Maybe	No
There are resources available to help you design your site.	Provide your own	Have resources on hand	Have resources on hand
You will need to provide a high-speed (high-cost) line to the Internet.	Yes	No	No
You will need to provide computers and technical people to manage the computer and the site.	Yes	No	No
You will need experience developing and supporting online purchasing services.	Typically none	Can range from experts to new in the business	Generally very new in the business

you will be told which secure server software, digital authentication service, electronic payment system provider, and merchant software it runs. Review the choices to make sure that the ISP provides you with the flexibility and scalability to meet your needs. The ISP will provide you with a client version of the software it is running.

2. *Hardware support*—Your online purchasing application must run on a secure server. Ask the ISP what technology it supports and what its management and backup procedures are. Find out what type of machines the ISP runs. Most ISPs run high-end UNIX-based machines. Make sure the ISP has the horsepower to support your transactions. Ask the ISP for the names and web addresses of customers running a large online purchasing site (by transaction numbers). Find out how many transactions per hour the site's computers can support and what its current load is. Visit the site to ensure that the online purchasing site works fast.

3. *Network support*—Make sure the ISP you choose has the network speeds to support your online commerce site. You should ask whether your online purchasing server is located on its own fast line, and find out how many servers are supported on each line. A good rule of thumb is no more than six purchasing sites per machine. You will also want to know the average connect time other e-commerce applications running on the server have. It is better to be on a server where the connect time is faster within seconds, since the server can handle more transactions per hour. Ask what happens if your transaction usage increases exponentially. Ask about the ISPs procedures for making sure your customers have 100 percent access to the secure server. You will be responsible for identifying your customer transaction usage. What you want from the ISP is a fast response; if you identify a surge in transaction usage and need to move to a large system, make sure the ISP has larger systems available for you before committing to using its secure server.

4. *Experience*—E-commerce is hot. Make sure the ISP you choose is experienced and has a track record running e-commerce services that support many transactions per hour. If it does not, ask for a reference list. You do not want to be the first e-commerce site this ISP has installed.

Go to the online purchasing sites of a few of the companies the ISP hosts. Buy a product. See if you like the response time and flow of the online purchasing procedures. Call a company that hosts its online purchasing service on the ISP. Ask to speak to the person responsible for working with the ISP and find out about her experience. Remember that your company's revenue depends on this provider. Ask the references if the ISP has had problems with outages (when the online purchasing site is not available) or if it has had complaints from customers regarding the responsiveness of the site.

If the ISP has not installed large enough lines or is supporting too many customers over its current lines, your site will respond slowly and your customers will think you are unresponsive. This will result in lost sales. While online adult sites are controversial, they were some of the first online purchasing services found on the World Wide Web. Sex sites are designed to support many transactions. An ISP that has been supporting sex-related sites most likely has online purchasing experience and high bandwidth capabilities. An ISP with sex-related customers tends to be a solid choice for hosting an online purchasing site. Remember that ISPs don't ask and don't review the content of their customers' sites. They see sites from the perspective of transferring bits of data between servers over the Internet.

5.3 What are your options if you don't want to host a site in-house but you have specific needs?

Some companies have specialized needs for a secure server.

Specialized needs might include running applications that are not commercially available:
- Auction software
- Providing partners with access to secure data
- Running a homegrown application

There are two possible solutions for companies that don't want to host an online purchasing site in-house but have specific needs:

- Cohosting
- Renting space on an SSL server

Tell Me More

If you want to provide applications that are not standard for ISPs, like auction software or specialized data, or your company has created an application you want to provide over a secure server, there are ISPs that support specialized applications. The first solution is cohosting; the second is renting space on an SSL server. Both of these options fill specialized needs. They are good solutions if you can't find standard merchant software to support your needs but don't want to be responsible for hosting and managing online purchasing within your company. Not all ISPs support these options. You will need to work closely with the ISP to make sure that the software you want to run works with its software and hardware. You will also need to identify how problems with the software and hardware can be resolved.

Cohosting—Cohosting is when you place your computer with your software in the ISP's facility. This provides you with its high-speed lines and twenty-four-hour management while you have complete flexibility regarding the applications you want to run. The caveat is that you need to make sure the ISP has the expertise and people to manage your system.

Renting space on a secure server—You may have an application that needs the security of a secure server but you do not have the in-house resources to manage this type of hardware and software. Some ISPs will let you place your software on one of its secure servers. This is referred to as renting space on an ISP's secure server.

5.4   How much does it cost to manage an online purchasing site with an ISP?

Each ISP has its own way to price hosting and services. The basics of pricing are:

- Onetime start-up costs
- Monthly costs

- Design/development costs
- Support costs

Tell Me More

Each ISP has its own cost schedule. Costs vary depending on the ISP and the service level you are interested in receiving. An ISP should, at the very least, have a good track record with online purchasing, 24 X 7 support, the ability to support large transaction numbers, and a competent support staff. Here is an example of what one ISP charges:

1. Basic service costs
   - $75 set-up charges
   - $50 monthly fee for up to 50,000 web hits (note: not transactions but hits). This includes 25MB of disk or an additional $110 a month for 100MG of disk space
   - A $1,295 one-time charge for a client version of the merchant software
   - Payment processing service start-up fee of $199 to $250 plus transaction fees
   - VeriSign certificate registration shared with up to six other merchants

   This translates into a $1,620 start-up fee and anywhere from $50 to $110 a month service charge, not including transaction fees.

2. High-end service costs
   - $350 set-up charges
   - $200 a month for 100,000 hits to $775 a month for 175,000 hits and 100 MB of disk space
   - $1,295 one-time charge for a client version of the merchant software
   - Payment processing service start-up fee of $199 to $250 plus transaction fees
   - VeriSign certificate registration fee of $395

   This translates into a $2,290 start-up fee and anywhere from $200 to $775 a month service charge, not including transaction fees.

Other costs might include creating and hosting a new domain and more-than-basic help with the creation of the online purchasing site. If you are expecting to receive hundreds to thousands of customers (unique visits) a day and have a large product line, you will need more disk space and more bandwidth. Your ISP will charge accordingly. You can start with the basic program and increase your services as your needs expand.

Choosing the level of service you want—Most ISPs have different service options you can choose. The three most common levels are:

1. Full service—access to high-end merchant software and the ISP's online shopping and online purchasing design team. ISPs that offer e-commerce design support will charge you by the hour or by the project.

2. Medium service—You have access to all the higher-end software and high-speed connections, but you need to design the site yourself or independently hire someone to create the site.

3. Basic service—Access to lower-end, less feature-rich software, and fewer services.

5.5 What are the basic tasks when setting up an online purchasing service?

Regardless of what service you choose, you will need to manage the setup of the site. Here is a list of tasks:

1. Design the online purchasing site.
2. Identify a bank.
3. Register with a payment provider.
4. Register for digital certificates.

Tell Me More

When you hire an ISP to host your online purchasing site you will need to design your site and register it with a few services. Here is a list of activities you will manage:

1. You or someone you hire will need to **develop the online ordering screens**. The merchant software on the ISP consists of blank screens. You will need to input your site's navigation elements and your products, including SKUs (bar code numbers) and cost, pricing, and tax. Check with your state regarding sales tax. You pay sales tax based on the state where your headquarters is located. A company located in California will need to charge California customers California sales tax. If your county has an additional sales tax, you will need to charge residents of your county accordingly. Make sure your merchant software has a pull down menu with options for sales tax.

2. **Identify a bank that supports online transactions**—You will need to register with a bank that supports online transactions. The bank will need to provide you with a Merchant Identification Number (MID) and a Terminal Identification Number (TID). Your ISP can provide you a list of banks with which it works. You will be responsible for registering your company with the bank.

3. **Register with a payment processing service (Cybercash, PaymentNet, etc.)**—You will need to register with the service your ISP is working with and provide the service with your MID and TID. Most payment processing services have an online registration site. It takes about fifteen minutes to fill out their form.

4. **Register for digital certificates**—Do so with a company such as VeriSign. Your ISP will provide you with the technical information to register with a digital certificate company. They will provide you with the web site of the digital certificate company where there is a form that needs to be completed. You will need to provide the digital certificate company information on your business. Companies like VeriSign will run a Dunn and Bradstreet credit report on your company.

5.6 What is the process for hosting online purchasing within your company?

If you decide to host an online purchasing site internally, you will be responsible for the entire process of developing, implementing, and maintaining your site. The tasks can be broken down into:

- Identifying available people with the time and technical skills to support and manage the web server.
- Choosing or designing merchant software that meets your needs.
- Setting up a digital authentication and payment system.
- Identifying and installing a telecommunications network sufficient to supporting site traffic for online purchasing.
- Creating and maintaining a secure environment.
- Ensuring that your online services are backed up and available. If the system crashes, you will need to have a backup system ready to support your customers.

Tip: Contact your accounting software vendor when looking for merchant software.

Tell Me More

The most important step for the successful creation of a internal online purchasing site is to identify and designate people within your organization who will be responsible for your e-commerce solution. Once you identify and create an e-commerce team, you need to have the team plan, identify, and integrate the components into a successful solution.

The first component that the team needs to look at and select is merchant software. You will need to evaluate merchant software to make sure it fits in with your environment. Start with your accounting software vendor. If they have developed merchant software, you will have an easier time integrating it with your existing applications. If you can't find software that meets your needs, you will need to architect, design, and develop your own solution. This is a considerable undertaking and should not be gone into lightly. Other software you will need to buy, install, and support is SSL or S-HTTP software to make your computer secure, digital authentication software to protect transactions, and electronic payment software. When you are ready to release your online purchasing site, you will need to register with the digital authentication and electronic payment companies.

Once you have identified the software, you will need to buy computers and networking equipment to support the site. Make sure you do not underpower your site. Customers who visit a site that is not working, or is slow, will leave. It is difficult to get them to return. Plan for growth and make sure you identify how you can quickly (within twenty-four hours) upgrade your system to handle loads larger then you expected. Security is important. You should have a security plan that clearly identifies how you have separated your Internet site from the rest of your computers. Since the Internet is 24 X 7, you will need to have 24 X 7 access to your site. This means you will need to have redundant backup computers and phone lines in case your primary lines go down. You will also need to make sure your IS people are available 24 X 7 to manage and support an around-the-clock environment. Europeans and Asians are awake while Americans sleep. If you are going after an international market, you will need to provide them with access to your site during their business hours.

5.7 How much does it cost to host your e-commerce site internally?

Internally supporting an online purchasing site should be reviewed and budgeted carefully. You need to budget the following:

- Onetime start-up costs
- Monthly costs
- Design and development costs

Tell Me More

If you are hosting a web site internally, there are a number of activities that you will need to manage. You will need to purchase and manage the computer hardware; purchase, integrate, and manage all the software components; and provide a network infrastructure (telecommunications lines) to your ISP, which will provide you with direct access to the Internet.

Hardware—The amount of computing power you will need is dependent on the number of customer transactions you expect per day. If your computing power or line speed is too small, customers will not be able to access your secure server, causing business to turn away. Most online purchasing applications run on UNIX- or NT-based systems. You can buy a PC for as little as $1,000 but most companies running online purchasing sites find that they need robust UNIX servers that can cost upward of $50,000. When you decide on the software solution, the vendor can help you identify what size computer to use. The size of a computer is based on the number of simultaneous transactions that will be supported; this is referred to as TPS—transactions per second.

An underpowered system will result in slow processing. Potential customers will become annoyed and leave your site. It will be very difficult to regain their trust and bring them back. Remember, it is said that a dissatisfied customer tells ten friends and a satisfied customer tells one. An underpowered system will not give you a successful hit.

Software—You will need to carry out the following software tasks for an internally managed e-commerce server:

1. Purchase and install SSL software on a computer.

2. Purchase or create an online merchant system.

3. Identify a bank that provides online transactions. Register with this bank and have them provide you with an MID and a TID.

4. Register and purchase software from a payment processing service (Cybercash, PaymentNet, etc.). You will need to provide it with your MID and TID.

5. Register, purchase, and install digital certificate software with a company like VeriSign.

Network infrastructure—Companies that host their own online purchasing site need a sufficiently powerful connection to their ISP. Your ISP will provide you with access to the Internet. If the connection to your ISP is too small, customers will not be able to access your service and will leave your site unhappy. For an e-commerce site, you need at least a T1 line. T1 lines start at $500 a month. The price depends on how far your office is from the phone company's central office.

Management—Don't underestimate the level of skill it will take to have someone manage and optimize your server and phone lines. Since your revenue is based on the system being available, you will need to have people on call twenty-four hours a day to have the system working.

5.8   How do you choose a turnkey provider?

As e-commerce grows in significance, many companies will begin providing full-service turnkey online purchasing services. These services can host your web site, host your incoming 800 number sales center, and even host your fulfillment functions. You will need to choose a turnkey provider that has the experience and resources to meet your needs.

- Working with a call center
- Working with a fulfillment house

You will still need your own online shopping site.

Tell Me More

As e-commerce grows in significance, companies that have not traditionally provided online services will begin entering the online purchasing business. The two most notable are automated call centers and fulfillment houses.

Many companies have outsourced their call centers. Call centers are the organizations that answer customer questions and process 800 number phone call orders. Over the last fifteen years, automated call centers have changed how businesses interact with their customers. Many companies provide their customers with an 800 number to order products. Some companies have decided to outsource this aspect of their business by hiring automated call centers to answer the phones and provide their customers with a way to get information and order products. Service companies see e-commerce as a natural service to offer. If you currently outsource your call center and plan on extending your current services over the web, you may decide to check with your call service vendor to see if it offers e-commerce support. If you decide to have your call center support your online purchasing site as well, you will need to make sure the call center has the resources and experience to handle online support and purchase fulfillment.

You can consolidate the number of channels customers need to talk to by hiring a call center to manage your online purchasing site. This way, the same channel processes an order, regardless of whether the request originated from a phone call or from an online purchasing service.

Remember that call centers are very new to the online purchasing business. They tend to work with a local ISP to provide online purchasing services to their customers. They will charge you management fees to develop your online purchasing site. You may be paying management fees to teach their employees how to create e-commerce sites.

Before choosing a call center to develop, host, manage, and support your site, do your homework and check out other online purchasing sites the call center has developed. Talk to people at these companies who are responsible for working with the call center. Make sure the call center has the resources needed to help you create an online purchasing site. Look at the software and services it provides. Make sure the look and features give you what you need to create a successful service. Make sure the call center has more experience than you have building an online purchasing site.

Fulfillment houses—Many companies have outsourced the distribution and shipping of their orders to fulfillment houses. For example, a manufacturer may send a pallet of its product to the fulfillment house. The manufacturer will then send its customers' orders to the fulfillment house, which will package and ship the products for the manufacturer.

Sometimes the fulfillment house can be responsible for some part of the manufacturing or assembly process. For example, a software company might send a master of its CD and documentation to a fulfillment organization along with the CD's external packaging. The fulfillment house presses the CD and prints the documentation, then creates packaging and ships the product to the customers the manufacturer has identified.

Fulfillment houses have recognized that providing their customers with online purchasing sites is a natural extension of their service offerings. They can integrate shipping products with online purchasing, providing fast turnaround for customers.

The same cautions that apply to call centers apply to fulfillment houses that claim they can create and manage your online purchasing site. Fulfillment houses usually are new to this business and may not have the expertise or flexibility you need. Investigate other online purchasing sites the fulfillment house has developed for its customers. Talk to the people in those companies responsible for working with the fulfillment organization. Make sure the fulfillment house has the resources and experience needed to help you create a successful online purchasing service.

Integrated call centers and fulfillment houses—Some larger companies have call center and fulfillment divisions. If your product fits with their business model, they can provide you with a full turnkey online purchasing solution. This would include customer order entry (either with an 800 number, an online purchasing site, or both), processing the order, and filling the order. Large national companies that currently have call center and fulfillment divisions are Rand and Softbank. Both companies, for a fee, provide their customers with many services.

You should not delegate your online shopping site to a turnkey provider—it is too important to your company. You need to maintain your online shopping site so you can quickly and easily update your product information and any other items necessary for an effective interface to your customers.

5.9   What is the process for working with a turnkey provider?

You will need to supervise the process to ensure it meets your company's needs.

- Provide pricing and product information on your product.
- Manage the execution to ensure it meets your requirements.
- Provide ongoing management to ensure quality levels.

Tell Me More

Working with a turnkey provider is like working with other vendors. You need to closely manage the process to get the results you want. At first, a turnkey provider does not understand your company or your customers. You will need to provide solid information and supervise her decisions closely, so she can develop a method that is successful.

Meet with your turnkey provider and explain your needs. The turnkey provider will register and set up your online purchasing site, including credit card transactions and digital authentication. You will be responsible for establishing the bank account to receive payments. Your bank will provide you with the TID and MID. You will give these numbers to your turnkey provider.

Verify that the turnkey solution provides you with an online purchasing system that integrates smoothly with your current web site. This ensures that the turnkey provider has the flexibility to work with your existing designers to incorporate your site's design elements. Monitor your online purchasing site closely to make sure it works correctly. You should be the one to confirm that your product pricing, delivery status, and description are displayed accurately. Make sure that the shipping costs and handling terms include the services and costs you want to offer. Test the e-commerce site to confirm that customer order confirmations are accurate and timely.

If you are currently using the turnkey company as both your call center and fulfillment support, expect to pay an additional charge for online support. The turnkey company will add a new section to your status reports, identifying the sales that came in by phone and those that came from the online purchasing site.

5.10   How should you manage the development of your e-commerce site?

Since e-commerce crosses functional areas, it is necessary to appoint staff from multiple areas to work together as a cross-functional team.

- A project manager should have the authority and responsibility to give the direction and installation of the site.
- Each department that will be affected by the creation of e-commerce applications should appoint a responsible member to the team.

- You must provide project team members with the responsibility and authority to make decisions.
- The team must develop a comprehensive project plan with clear targets, dates, and people assigned to each task.

Tell Me More

To create an effective e-commerce site, you will need to identify a point person to be the project manager. The project manager should have the authority and the responsibility to be able to obtain resources to create a successful e-commerce service. The project manager should be knowledgeable of company policies, products, and customers. She should have a clear vision of what e-commerce can do for the company. Skills for successful project management include the ability to prioritize, work with staff, lead people, set goals and direction, locate problems before they arise, and work within the system.

Identify people from the associated cross-functional organizations to be on the e-commerce project team. They should be empowered to make decisions for the departments they represent. The departments represented probably will be finance, information services (IS), MarCom, marketing, operations, and sales.

The project manager is responsible for creating the business plan. In chapter four we laid out goals, phases, and deliverables within each phase. Team members represent the organizations responsible for developing phase deliverables. They need to provide the project manager with their schedule regarding the execution of each task. The team manager will need to create an integrated schedule that identifies each task, elapsed time for each deliverable, prerequisites, and team member/department responsible for each task. The team will be responsible for managing the creation of the e-commerce service.

Here is an example of a project plan that was used to facelift a web site, develop a training tutorial, and develop an online purchasing service.

#	Task	Projected # of Days	Start Date	End Date	Prede-cessor	Resource
	Marketing	**38 days**	**12-Mar**	**4-May**		
1	Identify and register site with a bank	25 days	12-Mar	15-Apr		Executive, Project Manager
2	Main page new look	3 days	12-Mar	16-Mar		Web Designer
3	Review/ approve new look	2 days	17-Mar	18-Mar	3	Marketing VP
4	Update entire site	7 days	19-Mar	29-Mar	4	Web Designer
5	Review site update	1 day	30-Mar	30-Mar	5	Marketing VP
6	Create online store	10 days	30-Mar	12-Apr	4, 5	Web Designer
7	Review and approve online store	1 day	13-Apr	13-Apr	7	Marketing VP
8	Create online tutorial	16 days	12-Mar	2-Apr		Product Manager
9	Review and approve online tutorial	1 day	5-Apr	5-Apr	9	Marketing VP
10	Create press release for online tutorial	20 days	12-Mar	8-Apr		MarCom
11	Create press list for online tutorial	15 days	12-Mar	1-Apr		MarCom

#	Task	Projected # of Days	Start Date	End Date	Prede-cessor	Resource
12	Press launch for online tutorial	5 days	28-Apr	4-May	12, 10, 44	MarCom
13	Create product list for online purchasing	5 days	12-Mar	18-Mar		Product Manager
	Operations	**16 days**	**12-Mar**	**2-Apr**		
14	Identify e-commerce safety stock	6 days	19-Mar	26-Mar	14	Operations Manager
15	Identify inventory space	5 days	19-Mar	25-Mar	14	Operations Manager
16	Identify inventory resources	5 days	19-Mar	25-Mar	14	Operations Manager
17	Create e-commerce inventory	5 days	29-Mar	2-Apr	16, 17, 18	Inventory Manager
18	Identify shipping cartons	10 days	19-Mar	1-Apr	14	Fulfillment Manager
19	Finalize shipping procedures	1 day	24-Mar	24-Mar	28	Fulfillment Manager
20	Identify shipping resources	5 days	12-Mar	18-Mar		Shipping Manager
21	Identify accounting project resource	4 days	12-Mar	17-Mar		Finance Executive

#	Task	Projected # of Days	Start Date	End Date	Prede-cessor	Resource
22	Train accounting resources	3 days	12-Mar	16-Mar		Fulfillment Manager
	IS	**23 days**	**12-Mar**	**13-Apr**		
23	Update shipping software	14 days	12-Mar	31-Mar		IS Developer
24	Check on-line pro-cessing data mapping	3 days	12-Mar	16-Mar		IS Developer
25	Demo SW-RMA, Ac-counting, Shipping, Freight	5 days	17-Mar	23-Mar	27	IS Manager
26	Decide to purchase SW	1 day	24-Mar	24-Mar	28	Finance Exec-utive
27	Actually pur-chase SW	8 days	25-Mar	5-Apr	29	IS Manager
28	Install SW	4 days	6-Apr	9-Apr	30	IS Manager
29	QA software	2 days	12-Apr	13-Apr	31	IS Manager
30	Set up sup-port phone number	1 week	12-Mar	18-Mar		IS Manager
31	IS training	3 days	6-Apr	8-Apr	30, 42	IS Manager
	Support—RMA/ Customer Service/RFC	**35 days**	**12-Mar**	**29-Apr**		

#	Task	Projected # of Days	Start Date	End Date	Prede-cessor	Resource
32	Identify RMA project resource	4 days	12-Mar	17-Mar		Executive
33	Create product return procedure	2.5 days	24-Mar	26-Mar	14, 28, 36	Support Manager
34	Identify RMA resources	5 days	26-Mar	2-Apr	37	Support Manager
35	Train RMA resources	5 days	2-Apr	9-Apr	37, 38	Support Manager
36	Create accounting credit card return procedure	5 days	16-Apr	22-Apr	2	Fulfillment Manager
37	QA accounting credit card return procedure	5 days	23-Apr	29-Apr	40	Fulfillment Manager
38	Identify service resources	4 days	12-Mar	17-Mar		Executive
	Launch Tasks	**15 days**	**14-Apr**	**4-May**		
39	QA e-commerce site and infra-structure	10 days	14-Apr	27-Apr	8, 10, 12, 19, 20, 34, 39	Team
40	Launch e-commerce site	5 days	28-Apr	4-May	44	Team

5.11   How do you manage a site once it is released?

After you design a site and publish it on the Internet, it is important to identify the people responsible for managing the site on an ongoing basis.

- Appoint a web editor who is responsible for overall site continuity.
- Identify an operations manager.
- Identify an Internet business development manager.

Tell Me More

Most companies have found that web sites have a life of their own once they are launched. Many companies whose web sites started small quickly found their sites growing to over 1,000 pages. Most web sites start out working well and quickly become chaotic when the company falls into bad habits. Bad habits include:

1. Maintaining pages with links that no longer go anywhere, leading customers to dead ends
2. Maintaining pages that contain outdated or incorrect information
3. Changing the names (URL) of pages so people get 404 errors when they try to return to a bookmarked page
4. Not closely managing new page navigation
5. Not creating or enforcing page template standards and graphics standards

Web editor—It will be necessary for you to select a point person with the responsibility, authority, and time to manage your web site and e-commerce services. Without a dedicated, focused point person who is responsible for maintaining page consistency and site flow, your site will quickly become inefficient and unusable, causing it to become a customer repellent instead of a positive, new business channel.

This point person will be your web editor. Like a magazine editor, the web editor coordinates all web site activities and is responsible for site flow, integrating graphics and text into the site, and making sure the information within the site targets the chosen market. This position usually reports to the marketing organization.

The web editor should have excellent project management skills, show good attention to detail, be good at identifying and managing process flow, and have the interpersonal skills to work effectively with other departments. She will be responsible for maintaining quality standards for style, grammar, and spelling. She will need to enforce a series of page templates to ensure all pages have a consistent look, including page layout, navigation elements, and graphics. The web editor's responsibilities will include tracking site and user flow and managing all links. She will run a cross-functional team to track, approve, and publish any input or changes to the site by other departments.

If you currently have a web site but have not designated a web editor, you should identify one person when you begin creating your e-commerce services. Some companies use one person to be the e-commerce site project manager and a different person to be the web editor. This decision depends on how the company is organized, the skill sets of employees, and the size and scope of your current web site. A web editor responsible for a large web site will not have the time to manage the coordination of a new service such as online purchasing, though she should be involved in the process.

The web editor will establish and run a weekly cross-functional team. The purpose of this team is to track and manage requests for changes and improvements to the web site and e-commerce service. The team needs to decide how to handle each request and make sure that the subsequent change, if any, fits within the web site's flow.

Within your company, other departments will have primary responsibility for content creation, sales programs, support programs, and promotions. The web editor is responsible for aggregating this information into your web site. The organizations that should be responsible for and involved with the e-commerce services on an ongoing basis are sales, support, product marketing, and MarCom. Each of these departments will have responsibility for their respective tasks. For example, product marketing will be responsible for making sure the online shopping portion of the site provides the customer with the information he needs to make an informed buying decision. Product marketing will also develop and update product content. Marketing will make sure outbound marketing programs are reflected in the web site. Sales will monitor and track orders. Support (or sales, depending on your company) will be focused on updating the site's FAQ.

Internet operations manager—Most likely you will need a manager within your operations organization to support e-commerce transactions. This manager should be responsible for overall e-commerce fulfillment response. If you are working with a fulfillment house, this person is the point person. He is responsible for ensuring that inventory order levels are accurate and that the fulfillment house is fulfilling orders in a timely and accurate manner. If you are managing fulfillment of e-commerce applications within your company, this person is responsible for ensuring that your inventory is being managed correctly, that orders are being processed and shipped correctly, and that customer support issues are being processed in a timely and efficient manner.

Internet business development manager—Many companies with an e-commerce site find that new channels of online distribution are available to them. These channels provide new income, opportunities, and challenges. They create relationships. They manage, service, and support online retailers and distributors and they create new programs for existing partners who have online sites. To expand your online channel, you should select an Internet business development manager. Seek a person from your sales organization with a strong background in account management and an understanding of how the web can facilitate business. That person will work with partners, business associates, online stores, and online portals to bring increased visibility to your company's products and web site.

5.12   What activities are involved in maintaining a web site?

Managing an active site takes planning and preparation.

- Identify the needs of your environment.
- Create scheduled meetings to plan for new and changing content.

Tell Me More

The frequency of web content meetings will be based on the type of site you have and how fast information on your site changes. Web editors who work for companies with constantly changing sites work like television or newspaper editors. In this quickly changing environment, the web editor holds daily meetings with his staff of writers and technicians. This differs from a site that is more static. A web editor responsible for a static site may only need to run weekly or biweekly meetings.

Companies that have fast-changing web sites organize them to accommodate changing data. They identify an overall flexible architecture and maintain navigation elements within this architecture. Changing information is served from databases into the different elements of the page's consistent format.

In a fast-changing environment, the web editor has a team of people, each responsible for a series of tasks. The web editor establishes logical procedures and uses high-powered software to exert control over web site content and to add constantly changing information. News channels like CNN and CNBC, portals like America Online and Yahoo!, and product sites like Amazon.com are all examples of such sites.

Most companies have web sites that change at a slower pace. Many changes are known well ahead of time and should be anticipated; at most companies, weekly site-planning meetings work well. Departments or product managers that need to update the site attend these meetings. The Internet provides a company with the ability to make changes to its site instantaneously. The site-planning meeting is for planned changes. The web editor will need to set up a procedure with the content creator in order to manage the constantly changing pages.

When your company launches a new product, the product manager will create a list of new product pages. He will meet with the web editor to integrate these new pages seamlessly into the existing web site. During the week of the launch, press releases, news stories, and customer testimonials will be generated. The web editor will need to plan where this type of information will go. This will include creating appropriate navigation elements and links. As the information is created, the product manager will pass web pages with the stories for publication to the web editor.

A company that has static products but changing prices may find that product information may change yearly, while pricing information may change frequently. The web editor can create a procedure with the person(s) responsible for updating prices. The flow may work like this: The person responsible for prices updates the pricing page and e-mails it to the web editor. The web editor reviews the page for consistency, then publishes the page to the web site. If the pricing is extremely dynamic, they will create a database application that works directly with the web page. A visitor to this web site will be viewing pricing data updated directly from the pricing database instead of from an HTML page.

If the public relations department produces many press releases, it needs fast access to your web site to post them. Depending on your environment, you may want to give them access to a press release section of your web site where they can post press releases without going through the standard web editorial process. Most companies are comfortable allowing public relations limited, direct access to the Internet, since all press releases are reviewed and approved for external viewing.

5.13   Chapter summary

The most important steps in creating an effective e-commerce site are the execution and maintenance of the service.

- You will need to understand your technological needs and your company's technological capabilities in order to identify where you should host your services.
- It is important to identify key people responsible for the execution of the site.
- You will need to provide these people with the authority to steer your e-commerce site in the right direction.

Chapter 6
Marketing an
E-Commerce Site

An important step in creating successful e-commerce services is to develop an effective site design and to know how and where you can market your site.

Subjects covered in chapter 6

6.1   What do customers want in an e-commerce site?

Customers are the final judges of your site's success. If your site meets your customers' needs by providing them with the information they want in a simple, straightforward fashion, they will treat your site as one of their primary sources for information and products.

- Online, customers are more interested in a convenient buying experience than in a visually stimulating site.
- Information should be focused on creating an experience that is simple, easy, and informative.
- Information pertinent to customers should be placed up front and center.

Tell Me More

In chapter one we discussed the four generations of web sites. In Generation one sites, companies reformat their current brochures and turn their sites into "brochures online." In generation two sites, content reflects corporate issues such as investor relations, company mission statements, and messages from the president. Visually, generation two sites have many large graphics and are difficult for visitors to navigate. Your goal is to create Generation three and Generation four sites. Generation three sites are focused on driving business-to-business and business-to-consumer transactions. They are visually simple, fast, easy to navigate, and focused on the specific needs of the person visiting the site. Generation four web sites are the future. They physically resemble generation three sites. The difference between the two is predominantly behind the scenes. Generation four sites are dynamically created and tightly integrated into the operations of the company.

When developing a site, you can spend thousands of dollars on aesthetics and niceties. Surveys have shown that customers are more interested in a convenient buying experience (rapid response, quick downloads, good organization, etc.) than on appearance. A survey done by Binary Compass Enterprise shows that when customers buy online, web site aesthetics are the least important aspect of the experience. Customers are interested in a convenient buying experience, not the look of your site. A simple site with clear, accessible information is more effective than a site with beautiful graphics, poor navigation, and little relevant information. The look of your site is important to your company because it reflects your image; it is less important to your customers. People are interested in a convenient and easy location to find products and get the information they need: pricing, selection, product availability, and on-time delivery. Secondarily, customers are interested in product information, customer support, and ease of use.

6.2   What does a successful site look like?

A successful site reflects your company.

- It reinforces your branding.
- It provides easy navigation.
- It provides straightforward access to information.

Tell Me More

Customers are coming to your site to get information or to purchase a product. They are not interested in the aesthetics of your site. You still need to be interested in the look of your site since it is your company online. Branding is the visual imagery you apply to your logo, brochures, products, and packaging. Branding visually defines you. Your web site should reflect your current branding. McDonald's brand is the golden arches, Coca Cola's brand is the white swirl on the red background. You don't need to read the label to know that a product came from McDonald's or Coca Cola; all you need to see is their brand image. To create a successful branding campaign, you need to apply your brand (visual image) to all visual aspects of your products, including your web site. To create a successful web site, use your branding images as the basis for your web design. Incorporate your current branding elements, including color scheme, into the design and layout of your web site. If your corporate colors are teal and yellow, use teal and yellow on your web site. Keep the visuals of your online shopping site and online purchasing site consistent with each other. Customers get confused if the design elements change; they don't know where they are and may not trust the service if the site physically changes when they move from online shopping to online purchasing.

Spend the time up front laying out your site for easy navigation. A poorly laid out site will confuse visitors. If it takes visitors more than three clicks to get to the information they need, or if it takes a page longer than twenty seconds to download, the visitor is likely to leave your site. Currently, most successful sites are using Generation three layout, which are top and side navigation bars to simplify information access. They use a top navigation bar for high-level access to subjects, for example, products, support, online purchasing, corporate information, and site maps. Larger companies or companies with diverse product lines will use the top of the page navigation to provide visitors with easy access to each of their products. On the side of the page, the navigation bar is used to access second-level subjects. If a visitor chooses "products" from the top of the page, the side navigation will display all the names of the company's products. A visitor can then click on the name of the product in which she is interested to get to the online shopping site dedicated to that product. The side navigation bar will then be updated with the information specific to that product line. The center of the page is available to display information on the product or subject. The top navigation should remain constant throughout the web site. The side navigation should change based on where the visitor is in the web site. This way, the visitor can easily access subtopics from the side bar navigation and quickly move to major subjects via the top navigation.

Links:
Web Design 101—*http://www.hotwired.com/webmonkey/html/97/05/index2a.html?tw=design*
Web Style Guide—*http://info.med.yale.edu/caim/manual/contents.html*

6.3   How should graphics be used on a web site?

Graphics can provide your site with corporate branding. They can show what a product looks like and how to use the product. To effectively use graphics you should:

- Keep graphics small. People don't have the patience to wait for large graphics to download.
- Use standard graphics so everyone coming to your site can download them easily.
- Avoid using features like video and audio that need plug-ins to work. Many companies don't allow plug-ins to be downloaded onto their corporate networks and many consumers don't know how to download plug-ins.

Tell Me More

Graphics have an important role on a web site. They can be used effectively to brand your web site (e.g., a graphic of your logo) and they provide visitors with a better idea of what your product is and how it works.

Graphics should be used sparingly. Avoid using large graphics and photographs since they take a long time to download. Too many graphics or moving images on any one page make the page visually distracting. People become annoyed and leave a site if there are too many moving images. Graphics should focus on helping the visitor get a better idea of your product. They should be used to clearly convey how your product works. For most products, it is important to provide visual images. The web-standard way to visually display your product is through image files known as GIF and JPEG files. GIF and JPEG are image file formats that all web browsers understand and read for graphics and pictures. GIFs are images that use less than 256 colors, making them small files providing fast downloads. They are good for illustrations. JPEGs are used when photographs or higher-definition images are needed. JPEG supports up to sixteen million colors. JPEG pictures can provide beautiful colors and fine detail but may take many minutes to download.

It may enhance your product to show it in motion. MPEG2 is a digital standard for video. MPEG2 runs on the Internet. For visitors and customers to run an MPEG2 video, they will need a plug-in. You should avoid using any feature on your web site that needs a plug-in. Many companies do not allow plug-ins on their corporate networks. Many consumers don't know how to download plug-ins. When you include a feature that needs a plug-in, you have just eliminated a high percentage of people from accessing this feature. If you need to show a product moving, you should use an animated GIF. Animated GIFs work like an old-fashioned nickelodeon machine: Designers create a series of pictures, each of which shows the object in a different position. The pictures are then grouped together and displayed in rapid succession, giving the illusion of movement.

Links:
Creating graphics for the web—*http://www.widearea.co.uk/designer/*
Creating high-impact graphics—*http://www.netscape.com/assist/ net_sites/impact_docs/index.html*
Optimize your graphics—*http://websitegarage.com/*

6.4   How do you create effective web copy?

Copy needs to be formatted differently for the web. People read differently on paper than they do on a computer screen.

- By breaking paragraphs into bullet points, people understand more.
- Using active words to describe your web services makes readers sound like they are integrated with your business.
- Basics like proper grammar, correct spelling, and links that work are an essential part of good copy.

Tip: Develop your marketing content for the web first by using bullet points.

Tell Me More

Web readability is an important component of web design. Studies have shown that unlike printed text, people will not read large bodies of text on a web site. Visitors obtain a higher comprehension of the material if the text is broken into bullet points. Generation one web sites were not effective, since brochures were reformatted for the web. Not only were the graphics of these brochure online web sites very large, taking a long time to download, but the product information was written for paper usage, making it difficult to read online. People read differently online than they do on paper. To create effective online information, it is necessary to provide that information in bulleted form. The following example, taken out of a newspaper, is considered highly readable for print, but difficult for the web. Taking the same text and turning it into bullet points increases the readability of the text for the web.

Newspaper Sample—"Southwest Bank of St. Louis cut its prime lending rate Thursday, citing concern over falling commodity prices and fears global economic woes may slow the economy. Southwest, a small bank often leading the way for changes in lending rates, reduced its prime rate to 8 percent from 8.5 percent."

Web Sample

Southwest Bank of St. Louis cuts its prime lending rate:

- It lowered its prime rate from 8.5 percent to 8 percent.
- It is a small bank that often leads the way in changing lending rates.
- It cited concern over falling commodity prices and fear that global economic woes may slow the economy as reasons for its change in rate.

The words used to describe your web site in brochures and within the site itself tell customers how you view your site. Active verbs make a site sound dynamic and proactive: "find," "buy," "update," "download," as compared to using nonactive words like "enter," "up," "down," and "top." In all your marketing activities and literature, refer to your web site using active verbs and treat it like a central part of your business.

Passive example: "Our product information can be accessed

from our web site, where we have examples of our product information and product specification sheets."

Active example: "You can find information on our products and
product specification sheets by entering our web site."

Don't forget the basics. Make sure your copy is grammatically
correct and does not include spelling errors. Before you publish a
page, make sure the links work. Periodically go back through your
site and test those links. There are sites on the Internet like Web
Garage that will run spelling and link verification tests for you.

Link: Tips for writers and designers—*http://www.dsiegel.com/tips/
index.html*

6.5   What data should be tracked on your site?

Information on visitor activities and your customer base should be
tracked from your e-commerce site.

- You can use statistical information to identify popular paths
  and entry points.
- You may find a Bermuda Triangle on your site—a page people enter, never to be heard from again.
- It is worthwhile to spend the time wading through all the
  data you get from the current site-analysis programs.
- Use a site search engine. It is a great tool for visitors to find
  information and an excellent tool for you to find the keywords people are searching.
- Sales from your online purchasing service can be used to
  gather information on customer buying patterns.

Tip: Save the words people enter into your site search engine.
Update your site using popular keywords people are searching.

Tell Me More

It is unrealistic to think that you will create a perfect online shopping site on the first try. To make your site more effective, you will
need to be proactive in tracking visitors and visitor requests. Most

ISPs can provide you with site-tracking tools. If you host your site on a server located within your company, there are quite a few site-tracking software products available on the market. Tracking flow on a web site is a relatively new need. Many of the tools available on the market today will provide you with a wealth of statistics. Getting solid information from all these statistics is not straightforward. Current tools are no more then three years old. It will take a number of years for these tools to include data-mining techniques, providing you with an incentive to use the tool. Currently, most of the people who use site statistics tools get many pages (or screens) of data telling them who came to their site, where they came from, where they landed, and where they went. It takes many hours of poring over these statistics to get usable information.

Knowing the downside of gathering statistics on your site should not preclude you from gathering those statistics. The reward of refining a site is well worth the pain of using immature tools. You can use these tools to track visitor patterns so you can streamline the navigation of your site. These tools will provide you with the knowledge of how many unique visits your site receives and the common paths people take. Tracking tools will tell you from what site people are coming. You might find that there is a link to your site you are unaware of or that one search engine is sending most of the people to your site. Tracking tools can also highlight problems on your site. You may find that you have a Bermuda Triangle: a page people enter, never to be heard from again. If you find a Bermuda Triangle, go to the page and check out what customers are seeing. It may be that you have a large graphic that frustrates people, or a link that sends people off your site. Your goal is to create a sticky site—a site on which people stay or to which they return.

Another tool for identifying customer patterns through your site is a site search engine. Located on your home page, this tool provides visitors a way to put in a keyword and get a listing of all documents on your site that contain this keyword. Not only does this tool help visitors on your site find the information they need, but it is also a wonderful tool for you to use to find popular keywords people use when coming to your site. Have all the words entered into your site search tool saved in a file. Once a month, empty the file into a tool that lets you sort words (a spreadsheet would work). Identify those words that are continually being entered. Use these words to update your site. Many times, companies use uncommon words to describe their products. This disconnect can lead to confusion and, ultimately, to lost sales. You will find that, over time, as you apply common words from your search tool to your web site, you will have fewer words entered into your search engine. This is a good sign; it shows that your site is becoming more effective.

Another source for statistical information is sales from your online purchasing site. Financial data such as customer billing and shipping information can provide you with knowledge of your customers' buying habits. You can track where the people buying your products are from, what products are of most interest to them, and whether certain products are selling better in specific regions.

6.6   How do you use a survey to capture data on site visitors?

Many marketing organizations want to know more about the demographics of the people visiting their site. Creating a survey is an easy and effective method of collecting information.

- Keep surveys simple. Use pull down menus and radio buttons to make it easy to answer and collect data.
- Ask only a few questions. People get annoyed if a survey takes too long.
- Provide giveaways to entice more people to take the survey.
- If you advertise your survey with a giveaway, you will get many people visiting your site to register just for that.

Tell Me More

Surveys are a good way to collect data about people visiting your site. If you have content that people are interested in obtaining, you can create a simple survey that people need to answer in order to get access to this information. Make surveys simple by keeping your questions to a minimum; in most situations, don't have more than five questions. Make the questions easy to answer by using drop down boxes or by using radio buttons. Figure out what the most important questions are and put those questions on your survey. Most people are reluctant to provide full name, address, telephone number, and e-mail address, because they don't want to be added to a mailing list. If you want to gather personal information, clearly state how and when you are going to use this information. It is best to leave personal information as an option.

Places you can put an online survey:

• You can include it as part of the fill-in form for your online purchasing site.

• If you have an industry report or something of interest that people want to download, have people answer a few questions before they can gain access to what they want.

• If your site is a portal or destination location, you can include a survey in a conspicuous place near where visitors use services.

To increase the likelihood that people will take the survey on your site (and to get e-mail addresses), you can include a free gift. You might have the survey run for two weeks and randomly provide gifts to five people who have filled out the survey. The better the gift, the more people will answer the survey. The caveat with a giveaway is that there are people who will go to any site and register just for the giveaway. If you give gifts that are appropriate for your audience, but you don't advertise them, you will have a higher percentage of people who are interested visitors to your site filling in the form. Learn on Net.com hosts a free web class for people new to the Internet. They wanted to find out the demographics of the people using this service. At the time of the first survey, they had about 500,000 unique visitors a month to their site. They created a ten-question survey asking people simple questions about gender, age group, years on the Internet, if they were connected at home or at work, and what region of the world they lived in. Within two weeks, they got about eighty responses. A few months later they decided to repeat the survey, this time randomly giving away a total of five free T-shirts to survey participants.

Within two weeks they had received a little over 1,000 responses. A few months after the free T-shirt giveaway, they decided to run the same survey randomly, giving away one $100 modem. They received more than 1,800 responses. If you need information on people visiting your site, a simple survey with an inexpensive gift is a good method of getting market information.

6.7   How do you create a portal or a destination location?

A portal is a central site where people go to find information. A destination location is a web site or a portion of a web site that draws people for a specific reason. Portals and destination locations are not the part of a site that includes online shopping or purchasing information. They can be broken into several categories:

- Search engines or central link repositories are portals.
- Sites that are a central source for specific information can be portals or destination locations.
- Sites that provide education on a specific subject are destination locations.

Tell Me More

A portal and a destination location are web sites or areas within a web site that draw visitors based on its content. Whereas online shopping sites provide information on products, a portal or destination location contains information, products, games, or other features that provide people with information not tied to a specific product. The goal of a company running a portal or destination location is to drive traffic to its site. Usually, a company uses this traffic to gain advertising revenue, become a central hub for a specific industry or interest group, receive press coverage, or entice prospects to its site.

Search engines are the best-known portals. These are the sites that people use as their launch point for web activities. The top portals (based on number of people visiting) are search engines like Yahoo!, Go, Excite, and AltaVista. People use these search engine portals as springboards to find information on the Internet. Large search engine web sites are not the only portals. On a smaller scale, there are many niche portals. The goal of a niche portal is to be the destination location for people interested in a specified subject. If you have a special interest or are in a specific industry, there might be a portal (web site) that is dedicated to that industry. Most niche portals are link repositories, providing information and links to other sources within the industry. Industry trade journals or trade organizations run many of the niche portals. Before the Internet, these trade journals or organizations were the unifying source for their respective industries to obtain information. Now, to maintain their status, the magazines and trade organizations have expanded to the Internet, providing industry information and web links.

Portals and destination locations can also be informational. People go to these sites to get specific information. Tom's Hardware (www.tomshardware.com) is an information portal. This site is for people interested in PC hardware. It contains reviews on all types of PC products. It serves a niche market: people interested in PC hardware.

Any type of company can create a destination location. Let's say your company salvages 1950s auto parts and sells them over the web. You could develop a section on your site where people who rebuild 1950s cars can display them. You can give awards for the best rebuilt cars. If people who are interested in 1950s cars find your site appealing, they will bookmark your site, and they will frequently return to see the latest cars and awards. Your site is now a vintage car destination location. You can capitalize on this traffic by creating a banner like "Parts for Your Favorite Car." This banner leads visitors to a customization form. The form can ask the visitor to specify model, make, and year of the car(s) in which he is interested. When a part from that make, model, and year becomes available, you can automatically generate e-mail from your inventory database to the person who signed up with your service.

Educational sites can also be destination locations. People go to an educational site to learn more on a subject. Online education can be an excellent tool for companies that are in a new industry, or that have a complex product. They are also used by organizations whose mission is to educate the public or provide a specific group with information. People who create educational sites believe that by educating their target market, the target market will view them as a credible source of information. The site will become "sticky" (people will stay and return to the site). While on the site people will review associated products, and purchase products. Media coverage is another reason for creating an education destination location. Learn on Net, Inc. sells web-based classes to businesses. They have created an award-winning free class on using the Internet. They decided this free class would be a good vehicle for them to show off their training methodology. They use the free class to get positive press articles and Internet awards. They leverage the awards they have won for creating excellent, free, online training, into an international reputation for creating quality online courses.

One thing for companies creating portals and destination locations to keep in mind is that the information must be of high quality and not like something you would hear on an infomercial. People and the press are savvy. If you create a destination location that is only propaganda for your products, you will not generate press articles, nor will you create a following.

6.8   How do you advertise an e-commerce site on the Internet?

Web advertising can be used to drive potential customers to your site.

- Banners are the most prevalent form of web advertising.
- You pay based on the page impressions (people going to that page) for the page on which your banner is located.
- Online advertising can be more effective than other media because you can be ensured people were on the page where your banner was displayed.
- Most web sites selling web advertising have you sign up for a three-month minimum.

Tip: Banners are more effective if they are changed every two weeks.

Tell Me More

Web advertising is typically done through banners (the headline advertising you see on the top of popular web sites) on major portals. The general rule for advertising is that the site needs over three million visitors a day. The top ten Internet sites are Yahoo!, Go, Excite, Lycos, AltaVista, Snap, HotBot, GoTo.com, Looksmart, and WebCrawler. Like print, television, and radio, Internet advertising charges are based on the number of viewers.

There are a few terms used in advertising that are important to know:

- **Click-through**—People who click on an advertising banner
- **Hits**—Number of times the server downloads a page or an image (this statistic should never be used to define the number of people on your site)
- **Page impressions**—Number of people who land on a web page within a site
- **Unique visits**—Number of unique people coming to a web site

Some companies find that advertising on the large portals provides access to a lot of people but not access to the right people. Many companies find that advertising on niche portals, informational sites, or educational sites that cater to their target market is much more effective. With banner ads, you pay based on page impression. There are a lot fewer page impressions on a niche portal site than on a major portal site. Advertising on a niche portal will cost less, while providing you with an audience that is better targeted. Major portals are combating this phenomenon by providing potential advertisers with access to pages based on the user's search criteria. For example, if a person on AltaVista typed in "metal fasteners," an advertisement for a metal fabricator will come up on the search page, providing the company that is advertising a higher chance of reaching its target market. This way, the company pays for advertising on pages focused to its target market.

Internet advertising provides more focus and better statistical feedback than other media does, because the interactivity inherent in web surfing filters the audience for those who have an existing interest in information related to your business. It is cost-effective since you pay based on how many people land on the page on which your banner is displayed. This is referred to as the number of impressions or eyeballs your banner receives.

Popular Internet sites have statistics on the demographics of their sites and the number of impressions for each page. Banner space is typically purchased for a designated number of pages and a specified length of time.

This is how web advertising works:

1. You buy banner space from a portal.
2. The site charges you based on how many people click on the pages on which your banner resides.
3. The more visitors to the page, the higher the cost for the banner.
4. Many portals, such as search engines, can dynamically select what banners to display based on user inputs.

The average number of click-through responses to a generic banner is 1 percent. Click-through refers to the people who enter a web page, see your banner, and click on your banner to obtain further information. Your advertising company can provide you with the information on web costs and sites that meet your demographic needs.

Typically, a banner that is displayed for three months will cost between $10,000 and $45,000. The average cost is $70 per 1,000 page impressions. Companies that monitor banner advertising have also noted that after about two weeks, a banner becomes stale (unproductive) and the number of click-through visitors dramatically decreases. Therefore, if you plan a three-month advertising campaign, you should include the creation of at least six different banners. This will ensure that you have enough material so that the banner real estate can be updated every two weeks. Most sites do not charge you to refresh your banner. You should include in your advertising contract provisions that the banners are changed every two weeks. You will receive a report from the site on which you are advertising. It will provide you with the number of visitors to the page your banner was running on along with the number of click-throughs. Use different banners on different sites to see which banners are most effective.

You can find out which are the most visited sites from www. hot100.com. This web site closely monitors the most popular web sites and classifies the popular ones based on visitor interest or site focus. In most situations, to be considered worthy of web advertising, sites need to generate at least 2,000,000 unique visits per month. Since web advertising is still very new, the information and prices will probably vary from those provided here.

The current focus for improvements in web advertising is increasing in the click-through numbers. Currently the industry average for click-through is 1 percent. This means that only 1 percent of those visitors who land on a page with a banner will click on the advertisement to obtain further information.

A note on managing banner response statistics: Like site statistics, you can collect a lot of data regarding your banners. There is currently a lack of tools that provide you with good detail on who is coming to your site, from what banner, and what they do when they get to your site. The sites on which you have banners will provide you with counts specifying the number of people who came to the page along with the click-through rate. On your side, your site statistic tools can provide you with a count of how many people came from a specific site. To get more details on patterns of people who click on a banner, you will need to have the banner link the person up to a unique page where you can place a cookie on his computer to monitor his progress. Since there is a need for better tools, this market hole should be filled in the next few years.

Link: Listing of top sites—*http://www.aaa.com.au/world/america/ pop.shtml*
Link: Glossary of advertising words—*http://www.247media.com/ resource/re_gloss.htm*
Link: Advertising discussion group—*http:// www.internetadvertising.org/*

6.9   How do you use data mining to increase the effectiveness of your site?

Data mining is an excellent tool for analyzing sales information and increase the effectiveness of your site.

- Data mining can be used to identify customer buying patterns and to provide incentives for customers to purchase complementary products.
- Companies can use complementary marketing to increase the effectiveness of banner advertising.

It's True: Streamline, an online grocery store that uses data mining, has a 15 percent banner click-through rate when compared to the industry average of less than 2 percent.

Tell Me More

In chapter three we discussed data mining. Data mining is a series of sophisticated tools that searches through large databases to identify useful information like industry trends and customer patterns. A common use of data mining is to identify customer buying habits. If you have an online grocery store, by using data mining, you may find that people who buy peanut butter usually buy grape jelly as well. You can use this kind of information to remind online customers to buy associated products. Tracking customer buying patterns and providing incentives or reminders to buy associated products can be a powerful tool to increase sales. If you are a manufacturer, you can provide incentives or highlight products for your distributors based on the product the distributor is buying today or has bought in the past. A manufacturer of cabinets also sells cabinet hardware. When a distributor comes to the manufacturer's web site to buy a cabinet, the site can automatically display popular cabinet hardware and trim pieces. By providing associated products based on your customer's past or current buying patterns, you can increase the revenue of each sales transaction.

Data mining lets you be more intelligent with your complementary selling offers. You might start off by showing all the hardware that goes with certain cabinets. After a period of time, and by reviewing your sales patterns, you might find that the majority of your customers order the same one or two hardware patterns with each cabinet style. You might also find that the majority of your customers come back to purchase wall screws. By refining your complementary selling techniques, you can show distributors the most popular associated products like hardware and wall screws when they choose a core product like cabinets. This should increase the likelihood of distributors purchasing complementary products on your site. What has been found is that by creating mass customization, specifically configuring services individually for the customer either by showing her popular associated products or by showing her products she typically orders, your customer's buying experience becomes easier and more personal. You derive an increase in sales, an increase in revenue, an increase in profit margin and the ability to provide customers with better, more personalized service.

Streamline (www.streamline.com), an online grocery store located in Massachusetts, has been using data mining to increase click-through sales. Streamline targets banner ads based on the groceries a customer chooses. If a customer is viewing poultry, a banner for a chicken stuffing mix might appear. Ads can be targeted based on demographics. If the visiting household has males over eighteen years old, and the customer is viewing toiletries, an ad for after-shave lotion may appear.

Streamline has found that this approach produces click-through response rates of up to 15 percent as compared to an industry average of less than 2 percent. By combining online shopping, advertising, and purchasing, Streamline can provide its advertising partners with statistics that include the number of customers who saw their ads, the number of customers who clicked through, and the number of sales that were generated from each ad. This not only increases the effectiveness of an ad, but provides advertising partners with direct feedback they can use to refine their advertisements and their placement.

EToys is an example of data mining online. The site etoys.com sells toys online. On the site, a visitor can choose "toy search." Using a pull down menu, the visitor can choose basic criteria such as the child's age, price range, and toy category. The eToys.com online shopping site then provides the customer with a list of toys

EToys providing customers with data mining

that fits his criteria, saving him the time and hassle of visiting a toy store for a child's gift.

6.10   How do you register your site with a search engine?

There are many free sources that can be used to direct traffic to your e-commerce site. The most popular are search engines.

- Registering your web site with a search engine is free.
- There are web sites that provide services to help you register your site with many search engines at once.
- There are some basic tools you can use to increase the effectiveness of your registration. They include using title bars on

your web pages, creating a descriptive paragraph describing your products or services, and inserting meta-fields on your main pages.

It's True: A KPMG survey found the most frequent method of finding a site was via word of mouth; next was search engines and directories; the least frequent was links from other sites (both free and banners).

Tell Me More

There are many free ways to make your site known and to entice people to visit it. The most popular and productive free way to get traffic to your site is to register with the different search engines. There are some tricks to getting the most out of registering your site with a search engine.

Search engines and directories use both automated and manual methods to obtain information on content found on other web sites. Each search engine has its own particular way of categorizing information. If you plan correctly, you can effectively register your site. For example, Yahoo! (*www.yahoo.com*) uses a manual method where so-called librarians classify and list your site based on the description you provide them. AltaVista (*www.altavista.digital.com*), on the other hand, uses automated search robots called spiders that visit your site and display listings based on the words found in your site's content.

To register with a search engine, you can either go to each of the search engines, find the page on its site that lets you register with its service, and fill in the form, or you can go to a free online registration service. The most popular free search engine registration service is Register It (www.registerit.com). Submit It (www.submitit.com) is a popular pay registration service where you can register with the top eleven search engines. These services provide a form for you to fill out. The service then automatically registers you with about one hundred different search engines.

To prepare to register your site, you should do the following:

1. **Title bars**—Each web page has a title that shows up on the top bar of a web browser. Some search engines display your site

based on the words in the title bar. It is a good idea to use descriptive words in your title bar. If you are selling 1950 car parts, use the descriptive heading "1950s car parts" in your home page title bar. On your page for Chevy parts, use the title "1950s Chevy car parts." Anyone who searches on the words "car," "parts," "Chevy," or "1950s" will get a link to your site.

2. **Descriptive paragraph**—Some search engines ask you to provide a descriptive paragraph of twenty-five to forty-five words. A good way to start is to create a list of all the words that might be used to describe your product or service. From this listing, you can write a paragraph that uses as many of these words as possible. This way, if someone searches on a keyword you used in your descriptive paragraph, the search engine will display a listing for your site.

3. **Meta-fields**—Some search engines use meta names. These are words embedded into an HTML document but not displayed on a web page. Certain search engines just visit the meta-fields in your site and search for words that match the keywords entered by their visitors. Place this meta field on your home page and any other main heading page. You may decide to change the meta field based on the page on which you place it. If you sell clothing, you might have one meta tag with each product category on your home page. The following HTML is an example of what you need to add to a web page to create a meta name:

<meta name = "keywords" content = "*This is where you place the descriptive words describing your product or service*">

4. **Opening paragraph**—Some search engines search the home or opening page of a web site for keywords. If you place a descriptive opening paragraph on your home page, you simultaneously help your visitors know where they have landed and help search engines to identify you.

Classifications—Some search engines ask you to classify your business. When you register, they will provide you with a series of pull down menus that you can use to describe your company. These pull down menus ask whether your business is a reference site, business site, non-profit organization, etc. You will need to look through their classifications to see where you best fit.

Link: *http://www.kpmg.co.uk/uk/direct/industry/ice/ewired/index.html*
Link: *http://www.submitit.com/*

6.11   How do you create link programs?

Links are free methods of bringing people to your site.

- You can create a reciprocal link program; you will link to a site if they link to your site.
- An educational or informational destination location can be an incentive for others to link to you.
- Associates programs, where you provide a commission to sites that bring you people who purchase your products, is another type of link program.

Tell Me More

Another free way to bring people to your e-commerce site is through links. Some sites will provide a link to your site if you provide a link to their site; this is referred to as a reciprocal link. You should have conversations with your business partners, trade organizations, and local governments to see whether they will agree to link to your site. Some sites don't like to provide links to other sites because they want to keep people on their own site. Niche portals are typically good places to go if you are looking at creating traffic to your site with a link. Usually you need to create a compelling reason someone should link to your site. If you have developed a good training class on your product or industry, you can have distributors link their customers to this training class. If you are a distributor, your manufacturing partners can provide links to your site for fulfillment.

   If you have created a destination location, you may want to create a button that partners can use as a graphic to link to your site. If you have developed a site that has good information on a specific subject, you can create an icon (graphic) or button that web sites can display on their site to link people to yours. This way they can take advantage of the content you have developed. Many times, companies will use these links on their Intranet to provide employees with access to informational sites. For example, human resources organizations can provide a link to a web site dedicated to methods of avoiding repetitive stress syndrome.

Another way to bring people to your site is through an associates program. An associates program provides other sites with a bounty for any sales that are generated from a link from its site to your site. Most merchant software supports associates programs. Amazon.com, an online bookseller, has a successful associates program. Any site can register with Amazon.com as an associate. They then display a listing of favorite books on their site, with a link to Amazon.com's site. Amazon.com in turn provides the site 10 percent of any sales revenue generated by a customer who entered Amazon.com's site from the associate's link. There are many ways you can use an associates program to generate traffic to your site.

6.12   How do you use the media to drive traffic to your site?

Many forms of media, including magazines, trade journals, newspapers, and TV have an online presence.

- You can use the press to generate leads to your site.
- A story on your company that is covered in a trade journal may also be published on the trade journal's web site.
- Trade journals are interested in covering your company if you are the first in your industry to have online purchasing, a new customer support feature, or an industry standard training class.

Tip: Make sure you provide your web site address to the press covering your company or products.

Tell Me More

The media, including newspapers, magazines, television, and radio, are all focusing efforts on the Internet. The media posts many of its stories on the web. Getting a story in print and on the web about your company, web services, or web offerings is a good way to bring new people to your site.

The media is a great way to bring traffic to your e-commerce site. If you are the first in your market to establish an e-commerce site, have a creative destination location, or integrate your e-commerce site with other aspects of your business, the press may consider you an interesting subject for a story. Newspapers, magazines, TV, and radio have all created web sites where they display their most recent stories. You can get a story in print and on the web about your company. This will bring new people to your site. Many magazines, trade journals, and newspapers print their articles traditionally and publish them on the web as well. If your company or products were discussed in a magazine, there is a good chance the article, along with a link to your site, will be published on its web site.

6.13   How do you integrate e-commerce with existing marketing programs?

The most successful sites are fully integrated into a company's direction.

- All of your planned marketing, sales, and support programs should include information about your web site and your e-commerce element.
- Add e-commerce to your lead-generation programs.
- Combine e-commerce with existing distribution channels.

Tell Me More

The most logical place to create site traffic is within your existing market. To have a successful site, you will need to integrate your web services into your company's direction and strategy. All the marketing, sales, and support programs you are planning should include information on your web site and on your e-commerce services. This way, it does not appear that your e-commerce site is a separate venture.

If you are already selling your product and have an ongoing advertising program, you should include your web site URL in the existing ads and product literature. You should educate people that they can now purchase either through your toll-free telephone number or through your web site. For example, an auto dealer might use print ads to generate leads to her car lot. She can also use these ads to draw people to her web site, where they can better filter the leads and set up test drive appointments. The goal is to bring more leads with higher selectivity (more targeted) to the dealership.

Include e-commerce information in marketing materials and include information on accessing and using your e-commerce site in all your printed and otherwise published materials. Integrate your print pieces with your web site. The same way that you include your phone number in your literature, include your web site address. You can add a simple tag line to your print pieces, such as "now you can even purchase online from our web site at . . ." Integrating your web site address with your advertisements, letterheads, business cards, brochures, and billboards will integrate these services with your company and increase traffic to your site. For many customers, it may be easier to remember a web site address than a phone number. You can simplify your design process by designing your print pieces with the web in mind. Create a uniform approach to all the visual elements of your materials: design icons, colors, and graphics that can be used both in print pieces and on your web site. This will give your web site and standard corporate services a unified look.

If you are planning lead-generation programs (sending out mailings, making telephone calls, etc.), make sure you include your web site address in materials created for the effort. You can give potential customers the option to choose whether they want to be serviced from your web site or through your traditional sales channels.

Take the time to provide a training class on your web site for your salespeople. Instruct your salespeople to train their customers on how easy it is to use your web site instead of calling your offices. Create a simple brochure that describes how to use your web site and how web features integrate with current business practices. You may show how a customer can now use a telephone, fax, or your online purchasing service to place an order. You should show that regardless of which method customers use, the order flows through to the same fulfillment organization. Combine this program with incentives that encourage your salespeople to train their customers on your online shopping and online purchasing services.

All of these ideas and concepts should help you achieve success with your e-commerce site.

6.14   Chapter summary

Marketing your e-commerce services is the key to building a strong Internet presence.

- The Internet differs from other marketing mediums in its use of copy, design, and graphics.
- You will need to use design elements to brand your site.
- Tracking people on your site provides you with key information necessary to create successful marketing programs.
- Advertising, search engines, link programs, and the press are all methods you can use to bring people to your site.
- Use your current marketing programs to increase web usage and integrate your e-commerce services into your corporate direction.

Glossary

Access Provider
A company that provides you with Internet access and, in some cases, an online account on its computer system.

Acquirer
E-commerce lingo for banks.

ActiveX
A programming language developed by Microsoft that can be used to make a web page interactive.

ADSL (Asymmetric Digital Subscriber Line)
A method of transmitting data over traditional copper telephone lines at speeds higher than are currently available. Data can be downloaded at speeds of up to 1.544 megabits per second and uploaded at speeds of 128 kilobits per second (which is why it's termed asymmetric). ADSL is well-suited to the Web, where much more data is sent from a server to your computer than you send to the server.

Agent
A type of software program that is instructed to go out onto the Internet and perform a specific function on behalf of a user.

Anchor
An HTML tag that marks a specific point in an HTML document as either the source or destination of a hypertext link. This allows you to create links from one hypertext document to another, as well as to different sections within the same document.

Applet
A small software application sent from the server and run on the client, typically in the Java programming language.

ASCII (American Standard Code for Information Interchange)
A seven-bit code that represents the most basic letters of the Roman alphabet, numbers, and other characters used in computing.

Associates Program
A program that a merchant sets up providing a referral fee to a site that brings customers to the merchant.

Attribute
An addition to an HTML tag that extends or qualifies its meaning. For example, you can extend the <IMG> (image) tag by including the ALIGN attribute, which lets you further specify how you want a block of text to line up with an image.

Backbone
A high-speed line or series of connections that form a major pathway within a network.

Banner
Space on a web page used for advertisements.

BBS (Bulletin Board System)
A system that lets people read each other's messages and post new ones. The Usenet is the world's largest distributed BBS. The term *BBS* is used to describe private systems, run by individuals, that often require membership.

Binary File
A file that contains more than plain text (i.e., photos, sounds, a spreadsheet, or a formatted word-processing document) in contrast to ASCII files, which contain only characters.

Bit (binary digit)
A bit is the smallest unit of data a computer can handle. Bits are used in various combinations to represent different kinds of data. Each bit has a value of 0 or 1.

Bitmap
An image made out of an array of dots.

BPS (Bits Per Second)
Abbreviation for bits per second. Bps is a measurement of how fast data is transmitted. Bps is usually used to describe modem speeds or the speed of a digital connection. Eight bits make up one byte.

BPS (Bytes Per Second)
A measurement of how fast data is transmitted within your computer. BPS is eight times faster than BPS.

Browser
A software program that allows you to view and interact with various kinds of Internet resources available on the World Wide Web.

Cache
Storing information or a web page temporarily on your computer.

Call Center
A facility where phone operators answer customer questions or take customer orders.

CD-ROM (Compact Disk Read Only Memory)
A storage medium for digital data. Currently CD-ROMs can hold 650 MB.

Collaboration Tools
An electronic means of allowing teams of people to share information, regardless of where they are located.

Common Gateway Interface (CGI)
An interface program that enables an Internet server to run external programs to perform a specific function.

Chat Room
An electronic space, typically a web site or a section of an online service, where people can go to communicate online in real time. Chat rooms are often organized around specific interests, such as small-business owners, gardening, etc.

Clickable Image
Any image that has instructions embedded in it so that clicking on it initiates some kind of action or result.

Click Through
Each person who clicks on an image like an advertising banner is considered one click through.

Client
A program that uses the services of another program. The client is the program used to contact and obtain data or request a service from the server.

Computer Virus
A computer program that invades computers and networks and wreaks havoc on them.

Cookie
A file placed on a web browser by a web server to record a visitor's activities on a web site.

Cryptography
The process of securing private information that is passed through public networks by mathematically scrambling (encrypting) it in a way that makes it unreadable to anyone except the person or persons holding the mathematical key that can unscramble (decrypt) it.

Cyberspace
A term coined by science fiction author William Gibson to describe the whole range of information resources available through computer networks.

Database
A structured format for organizing and maintaining information that can be easily retrieved.

Data Mining
Tools to create applications that access information a company has gathered on customers and products.

Destination Location
A web site that has compelling information on it. People visit destination locations to get specific information.

Dial-Up Account
A type of account available for connecting to the Internet. A dial-up account through an Internet Service Provider allows you to use your modem to make a connection to your provider's system, and the Internet.

Digital Authentication
A method used to authenticate that the server receiving the information is actually the correct server.

Directory
A system that your computer uses to organize files on the basis of specific information.

Disintermediation
The process of bringing a company closer to its customer by cutting out the information middleman.

Dithering
A technique to simulate the display of colors that are not in the current color palette of a particular image. This is accomplished by arranging adjacent pixels of different colors into a pattern that simulates colors that are not available to the computer.

Domain Name
The unique name that identifies an Internet site.

Domain Suffix
Designates on what network a specific domain name resides. For U.S. domains, the suffixes are:
    .com—corporations
    .edu—educational institutions
    .org—nonprofit organizations
    .mil—military organizations

.net—network providers
.gov—government institutions

In addition, non-U.S. sites have an additional extension that indicates the country where the domain is located. For example:

.au—Australia
.dk—Denmark
.de—Germany
.uk—United Kingdom

Download

The method by which users access and save or pull down software or other files to their own computers from a remote computer, usually via a modem.

DPI (Dots Per Inch)

A measurement of print image resolution and quality. A larger number of dots allows for more detail and, therefore, a higher-resolution image.

Electronic Checks

An electronic payment system whereby transfers are made from a client's checking account to a merchant's bank account.

Electronic Commerce (e-commerce)

A range of online business activities that includes explaining products and services and providing a mechanism for customers to buy those products and services from a web site. E-commerce encompasses online shopping and online purchasing.

Electronic Payment System

A means of collecting payments over the Internet.

E-mail (electronic mail)

Messages, often text, sent from one user to another via a network.

E-mail Address

A computer mailing address to which electronic mail may be sent. Each type of computer system handles e-mail addressing differently, but each relies on various protocols for exchanging mail with other, dissimilar systems.

Encryption

A way of coding the information in a file or e-mail message so that if it is intercepted by a third party as it travels over a network, it cannot be read.

Executable File or Content

A file that is a program. Executables in DOS and Windows usually have an .exe or a .com extension. In UNIX and Macintosh environments, executable files can have any name.

External Viewer
An additional piece of software that helps your browser interpret and display specific file types that it doesn't have the built-in ability to read.

Extranet
A network that allows a company to share information with other businesses and customers. Extranets transmit information over the Internet and require a user to have a password to access data from internal company servers.

FAQ (Frequently Asked Questions)
Online documents that list and answer the most common questions on a particular subject.

File Compression
A way of reducing the size of a file (or files) so that it doesn't take up a lot of space on a server or hard drive and can travel faster over a network.

File Permissions
A method of specifying who can access files and what type of access they can have.

Firewall
A form of security made up of a combination hardware and software buffer that many companies and organizations have in place between their internal networks and the Internet. A firewall allows only specific kinds of messages from the Internet to flow in and out of the internal network. This protects the internal network from intruders or hackers who might try to use the Internet to break into those systems.

Floppy Disk
Also called a diskette. This is the magnetic storage medium used to store and transfer data.

Forms
Web pages comprised of text and fields for a user to fill in with information.

FTP (File Transfer Protocol)
A common method of transferring one or more files from one computer to another.

Fulfillment House
A facility that picks, packs, and ships orders.

Gateway
Hardware or software that bridges the gap between two otherwise incompatible applications or networks so that data can be transferred among different computers.

GIF (Graphics Interchange Format)
A graphics file format compression scheme. A GIF is used to send and display graphic files over a network.

GUI (Graphical User Interface)
An interface that allows users to navigate and interact with information on their computer screen by using a mouse to point, click, and drag icons and other data around the screen instead of typing in words and phrases.

Hacker
Slang term for a computer user who enjoys exploring computer systems and writing computer programs. Hackers have received a bad reputation since some hackers like to make a name for themselves by breaking into web sites, company computers, or developing viruses.

Hit
A measurement of files that are downloaded from a web server. Hits are a way of measuring traffic to a web site that can be misleading. Each time a server downloads a graphic or text to a page, it is considered one hit. The number of hits a site receives is usually much greater than the number of visitors it gets. That's because a web page can contain more than one file.

Home Page
Also referred to as an Index page. The starting point of a Web presentation and a sort of table of contents for what is at the web site, a home page offers direct links to the different parts of the site.

Host Name
Every computer that is directly connected to the Internet has a numerical identification, called an IP address, and a name, called a host name.

Hotlist
A list of interesting, useful, or important URLs you can click on to go directly to a web site. A standard feature of most web browsers.

HTML (HyperText Markup Language)
The computer language used to create hypertext documents. HTML utilizes a finite list of tags that describe the general structure of various kinds of documents linked together on the World Wide Web.

HTTP (HyperText Transfer Protocol)
The method by which hypertext files are transferred across the Internet.

Hypertext
A way of presenting information in which text, sounds, images, and actions are linked together in a way that allows you to jump around between them in whatever order you choose. Hypertext usually refers to

any text available on the World Wide Web that contains links to other documents.

Icon

A small image, usually a symbol, used to graphically represent a software program, file, or function on a computer screen.

Image Map

A graphic divided into regions or hot spots. When a particular region is clicked, it calls up a web page that has been linked to that particular region.

Internet

A large group of computers that can be accessed via TCP/IP by anyone using a web browser.

Internet Technology

A group of standard technologies used to let different people using different technology share information. The underpinnings of Internet technology are TCP/IP and web browsers.

Internet Telephony

While the Internet was first devised as a way of transmitting data, it is now being used to make voice calls. By converting the analog speech signals used on current telephone systems into digital data, calls can be sent over the Internet, bypassing long distance charges.

Intranet

An internal Internet designed to be used within the confines of a company, university, or organization. Intranets are private; using Internet technology in a company makes internal communication and collaboration much simpler.

IP Address

A numeric code that uniquely identifies a particular computer on the Internet. Just as a telephone number identifies a telephone, an IP address identifies a computer on the Internet.

IRC (Internet Relay Chat)

A program that allows you to carry on live conversations with people all over the world by typing messages back and forth across the Internet.

ISDN (Integrated Services Digital Network)

Connections that use ordinary phone lines to transmit digital instead of analog signals, allowing data to be transmitted at a much faster rate than with a traditional modem. ISDN lines support two 64 KB lines or an aggregate of 128 KB.

ISP (Internet Service Provider)

Also called access providers. This remote computer system is one to which you connect your personal computer and through which you connect to the Internet (ISPs that you access by modem and telephone line are often called dial-up services).

Java
A hardware- and software-independent programming language that can be used to create Internet-based applications.

JavaScript
A scripting language that allows dynamic behavior to be specified within HTML documents.

JPEG (Joint Photographic Experts Group)
An industry committee that developed a compression standard for still images. JPEG refers to the graphics file format that uses this compression standard.

LAN (Local Area Network)
A local network of computers that is located on the same floor or in the same building or nearby buildings.

Link
A term that generally refers to any highlighted words or phrases in a hypertext document that allow you to jump to another section of the same document or to another document on the World Wide Web.

Login
The account name used to access a computer system. It is the way people identify themselves to their online service or Internet access provider. Login is also called User ID, User Name, or Account Name.

Lurker
A slang term for someone who regularly reads newsgroup, BBS, or mailing list discussions, but rarely participates in them.

Mailing List
A group of e-mail names used to distribute e-mail to a large number of people.

Mass Customization
A system that provides an individual visitor to your web site with information customized to his needs.

Merchant Software
Software used by merchants to create an online purchasing site.

Micro Payments
A form of electronic payment that is used for small transactions.

MID (Merchant Identification Number)
An identification number provided by a bank to identify the merchant in an e-commerce transaction.

MIME (Multipurpose Internet Mail Extension)
A standard system for identifying the type of data contained in a file based on its extension. MIME is an Internet protocol that allows you to send binary files across the Internet as attachments to e-mail messages. This includes graphics, photos, sound and video files, and formatted text documents.

Mirrored Site
Two servers that have the same information. A mirrored site is typically used as backup in case one server goes down.

Modem (Modulator/Demodulator)
A device that allows remote computers to transmit and receive data using telephone lines.

MOV
A file extension found on the World Wide Web that denotes the file is a movie or video in QuickTime format.

MPEG (Moving Pictures Experts Group)
An industry committee that is developing a set of compression standards for moving images (i.e., film, video, and animation) that can be downloaded and viewed on a computer.

Multimedia
The use of more than one type of media simultaneously: text with sound, moving or still images, music, etc.

Navigation Tools
Tools that allow users to find their way around a web site or multimedia presentation. They can be hypertext links, clickable buttons, icons, or image maps. Navigation tools are usually present at either the bottom or top (sometimes both) of each page or screen and typically allow users to return to the previous page, move forward to the next page, jump to the top of the current page, or return to the home page.

Netiquette
An informal code of conduct that governs what is generally considered to be the acceptable way for users to interact with one another online.

Network
Two or more computers connected to each other so they can share resources. The Internet is a network of networks, whereby anyone from an individual at home with a PC to a large corporate multidepartmental system can freely and easily exchange information.

Newsgroups
Electronic discussion groups consisting of collections of related postings (also called articles) on a particular topic that are posted to a news server

that then distributes them to other participating servers. There are thousands of newsgroups covering a wide range of subjects. You must subscribe to a newsgroup in order to participate in it or to track the discussion on an ongoing basis. Unlike magazine or newspaper subscriptions, subscribing to a newsgroup does not cost anything.

Newsreader
A software program that lets you subscribe to newsgroups as well as read and post messages to them. A newsreader is like a friendly librarian who keeps track of the articles posted to the newsgroups you like to read and locates them when you want to read them.

Node
An addressable point on a network. A node can connect a computer system, a terminal, or various peripheral devices to the network. Each node on a network has a distinct name. On the Internet, a node is a host computer with a unique domain name and address that has been assigned to it by InterNIC.

OBI (Open Buying on the Internet)
A standard built around a common set of business requirements and supporting technical architecture, specifications, and guidelines. The goal of OBI is to create a standard so companies can integrate their Intranet applications with different vendors' web-enabled applications.

Object-Oriented Programming
A programming technique that speeds the development of programs and makes them easier to maintain through the reuse of objects that have behaviors, characteristics, and relationships associated with them. The objects are organized into collections (also called class libraries) that are then available for building and maintaining applications. Each object is part of a class of objects, which are united via inheritance and share certain characteristics and relationships.

Online Account Reconciliation
Going online to pay your bill.

Online Purchasing
The technical infrastructure that makes it possible to actually purchase a product over the Internet.

Online Shopping
The breadth and depth of information and activities that provide the customer with the information she needs to make an informed buying decision.

Packet/Packet Switching
A chunk of information sent over a network. Packet switching is the process by which a carrier breaks up data into these chunks or packets. Each

packet contains the address of origin, the address of its destination, and information about how to reunite with other related packets. This process allows packets from many different locations to comingle on the same lines and be sorted and directed to different routes by special machines along the way.

Page Impression

A unit of measurement used for banner advertisement. Each unique person who views a page on a web site is measured as a one-page impression. Page impressions are the number of people who land on a web page within a site.

Parse

The process by which programming data input is broken into smaller units.

Password

A code or word used to gain access to restricted data on a computer network. While passwords provide security against unauthorized users, the security system can only confirm that the password is legitimate, not whether the user is authorized to use the password.

Pathname

A name that indicates the location of a particular file or directory by outlining the route or path from the host name (if the file resides on a remote server) through the directory structure to the desired file name or directory name. Each name in the series of names that defines a path is separated by a slash. If the file is located in the current working directory on your computer, it is referred to only by its file name.

PDF (Portable Document Format)

A file of type created by Adobe Systems that allows fully formatted, high-resolution, postscript documents to be easily transmitted across the Internet and viewed on any computer that has Adobe Acrobat Reader software. A proprietary viewer is available for free at the Adobe site.

PERL (Practical Extraction and Reporting Language)

A robust programming language frequently used for creating CGI programs on web servers because it is a script language that can read and write binary files, and it can process very large files. The major advantage of PERL over C as a programming language is that PERL does not need to be compiled.

Ping

A term and command used to test the Internet to see what systems are working. Ping can also test and record the response time of accessing other companies. This provides a systems administrator with valuable information on what networks are overloaded so that he can optimize access times.

Pixel (Picture Element)
The smallest element that can be displayed on a video screen or computer monitor. It is often used as a unit of measurement for image size and resolution. The number of pixels (width and height) in an image defines its size and the number of pixels in an inch defines the resolution of the image.

PKZIP/PKUNZIP
A software compression utility for a PC. It allows you to compress or zip a file or a number of files into one archive file in the ZIP file format. To decompress, or unzip the files, you use PKUNZIP, which comes as part of the PKZIP package. For Windows users, there is WinZip. Both PKZIP and WinZIP are available on many public FTP sites.

Plug-In
Extends the capabilities of a web browser, such as Netscape Navigator or Microsoft Explorer, allowing the browser to run multimedia files. The term *plug-in* is used in two ways on the Internet. The technical definition of a plug-in is a small add-on piece of software that conforms to Netscape Navigator standards. Explorer actually uses a different software standard, called ActiveX control, instead of plug-ins.

Pointer
A word, picture, or navigation element that, when clicked on, moves a user from one point in a document to another point or to another document altogether. It is the same as a link.

POP
An acronym for Point of Presence. A POP is the local telephone exchange from which you receive service.

POP Server
A server using the Post Office Protocol, which holds users' incoming e-mail until they read or download it.

Port
A connector on a computer to which peripheral devices, such as printers or modems, are attached. Typically, these are serial ports, parallel ports, and modem ports.

Portal
A key site on the Internet that most people visit (e.g., AltaVista, Yahoo!, America Online).

Posting
An electronic message posted to an electronic communication service, such as a newsgroup or BBS (Bulletin Board System).

PPP (Point-to-Point Protocol)
A communications protocol used to transmit network data over telephone lines. It allows you to connect your computer to the Internet itself, rather than just to your Internet Service Provider's host computer. This type of connection lets you communicate directly with other computers on the network using TCP/IP connections. It is part of the TCP/IP suite of programs necessary to connect to and use the Internet.

Presentment
A system that provides an online account reconciliation to your customers (i.e., the phone company providing an online listing of a customer's phone calls).

Private Extranet
Using Internet technology over private or leased lines. A private Extranet is a web site for specific customers or partners that can only be accessed over private lines.

Protocol
The standard or set of rules that two computers use to communicate with each other. Also known as a communications protocol or network protocol, this is a set of standards that ensures that different network products or programs can work together. Any product that uses a given protocol should work with any other product using the same protocol.

Pull Technology
Technology used to seek out and download information to your computer. This contrasts with push technology, where data is automatically delivered to your computer.

Push Technology
Technology that allows data to be sent automatically to your computer at regular intervals, such as news updates every hour, or when triggered by an event, such as when a web page is updated. Push technology has been touted as an alternative to the way the World Wide Web currently operates, where users go online to search for information.

Query
The process by which a web client requests specific information from a web server, based on a character string that is passed along. A query typically takes the form of a database search for a particular keyword or phrase. The keyword is entered into the search field of an Internet directory such as InfoSeek and then passed onto the web server.

QuickTime®
A file extension developed by Apple Computer Inc. for videos or movies (like animations) compressed using its QuickTime® format. When you

see the QuikTime® extension on the World Wide Web, it means that the file in question is a movie or video. If you want to play the movie after you download the file, your computer must support the QuickTime® format.

RGB Mode
A color model (Red, Green, and Blue) commonly used to display color in video systems, film recorders, and computer monitors. It represents all colors as combinations of red, green, and blue light. RGB mode is the most common color mode for viewing and working with digital images on a screen.

Robots
Software programs designed to automatically go out and explore the Internet for a variety of purposes. Robots that record and index all of the contents of the network to create searchable databases are sometimes called Spiders or Worms. AltaVista, WebCrawler, and Lycos are sites that use robots.

ROI
Return on investment—figuring out how much return a particular investment will pay back. The three most popular forms of ROI are:
- Cost Chain—tells how this service saves money
- Value Chain—increases service to increase sales or provide additional value
- Transaction Chain—reduces a process to save money

Router
Hardware that connects two or more networks. A router functions as a sorter and interpreter as it looks at addresses and passes bits of information to their proper destinations.

Script
A type of program that consists of a set of instructions for another application or utility to use.

Search Engine
A type of software that creates indexes of databases or Internet sites based on the titles of files, keywords, or the full text of files. A search engine has an interface that allows you to type what you're looking for into a blank field. It then gives you a list of the results of the search. When you use a search engine on the Web, the results are presented to you in hypertext, which means you can click on any item in the list to get the actual file. If the file you select doesn't have what you're looking for, you can use the back button on your browser to return to the list of search results and try something else.

Secure Server
Technology that ensures that the information a customer enters on an e-commerce site is encrypted and cannot be stolen.

Server
A computer that handles requests for data, electronic mail, file transfers, and other network services from other computers (i.e., clients).

Shareware
Software that is freely distributed for a small fee paid on an honor system. You are not required to pay the fee to try the program, but if you like the software enough to use it, you are expected to send the fee directly to the creator.

Shopping Cart
An icon that, when pressed, lets an online customer save the current product, allowing him to continue shopping on the web site.

Signature
Text automatically included at the bottom of an e-mail message or news-group posting to personalize it. This can be anything from a clever quote to some additional information about the sender, such as his title, company name, and any additional e-mail addresses he may have. Netiquette suggests that signatures be four lines or fewer.

SLIP (Serial Line Internet Protocol)
A communications protocol that, like PPP, allows you to connect your computer to the Internet itself, using a telephone line. It is part of the TCP/IP suite of programs necessary to connect to and use the Internet.

SMTP
An acronym for Simple Mail Transfer Protocol. SMTP is the protocol used for routing e-mail across the Internet.

SPAM
A term used to refer to the practice of blindly posting commercial mes-sages or advertisements to a large number of unrelated and probably dis-interested newsgroups.

SSL (Secure Socket Layer)
SSL is a low-level encryption scheme that ensures transactions over the Internet are secure.

Streaming Media
On the World Wide Web, typically you download a file to your computer, then you view it. This system works well with small files, but large multi-media files, such as video clips and audio, can take several minutes or longer to download. With streaming media, a file begins to play seconds

after it is received by your computer, because the media is delivered in a stream from the server.

String/Search String
A sequence of characters, words, or other elements that are connected to each other in some way. A search string usually refers to a string of words or a phrase that is used to search and locate or retrieve a specific piece of information contained in a database or a set of documents.

Syntax Error
The order in which words and phrases are put together, such as a URL (web address), which consists of several phrases strung together to define a location or service on the Internet. A syntax error occurs when a user (or programmer) has put words in an order that a program does not understand. A syntax error while surfing the Web may be caused by a mistyped or inadvertently rearranged URL, making it incomprehensible to a web browser.

T1 Line
A high-speed digital connection capable of transmitting data at a rate of approximately 1.54 million bits per second. A T1 line is typically used by small and medium-size companies with heavy network traffic. It is large enough to send and receive very large text files, graphics, sounds, and databases instantaneously, and it is the fastest speed commonly used; basically it is too large and too expensive for individual home use.

T3 Line
A super high-speed connection capable of transmitting data at a rate of 45 million bits per second. A T3 line represents a bandwidth equal to about 672 regular voice-grade telephone lines, which is wide enough to transmit full-motion, real-time video, and very large databases over a busy network. A T3 line is typically installed as a major networking artery for large corporations and universities with high-volume network traffic. The backbones of the major Internet service providers are comprised of T3 lines.

Tags
The set of descriptive formatting codes used in HTML documents that instruct a web browser how to display text and graphics on a web page. For example, to make text bold, the tags <B> and </B> are used at the beginning and end of the text.

TCP/IP (Transmission Control Protocol/Internet Protocol)
Protocol governing communications between all computers on the Internet. TCP/IP is a set of instructions that dictates how packets of information are sent across multiple networks. Also included is a built-in error-checking capability to ensure that data packets arrive at their final destination in the proper order.

Telnet
A software program that allows you to log into other remote computers on the Internet to which you have access. Once you are logged into the remote system, you can behave like a local user.

TIN (Terminal Identification Number)
An identification number given to a merchant by a bank to identify who the merchant is.

Turnkey Hosting
A company that provides services that include e-commerce, 800 number sales support, and fulfillment.

24 × 7
24 × 7 (twenty-four by seven) refers to having services available twenty-four hours a day, seven days a week.

Unique Visit
Unit of measurement used for web advertising; measures the number of unique people coming to a web site. Note: Every time a person leaves a site and comes back to the site, he is considered a unique visit.

Upload
Uploading a file means loading it from your computer onto a remote one. Most people do a lot more downloading than uploading.

URL (Uniform Resource Locator)
The address for a resource or site (usually a directory or file) on the World Wide Web and the convention that web browsers use for locating files and other remote services.

Use-Based Services
Services customers pay for based on how much they use them. Popular use-based services are utilities like phone, water, and electricity.

Usenet
A collection of newsgroups and a set of agreed-upon rules for distributing and maintaining those newsgroups.

User Name
Same name as your login. This is the name by which you and your electronic mailbox are identified online. A user name is also called User ID or Account Name.

Viewer
A software application or tool designed to display a specific type of file (usually one that contains something other than text) that your web browser normally can't display on its own. There are viewers to display graphics files and to play sound or video files.

VRML *(Virtual Reality Modeling Language)*
An open, platform-independent file format for 3-D graphics on the Web. It encodes computer-generated graphics in a way that makes them easily transportable across the network. VRML requires a special web browser to display these graphics, which simulate virtual reality, 3-D environments or worlds through which the user can move and interact with objects. These 3-D worlds can contain objects that link to documents, other objects, or other 3-D worlds.

WAN *(Wide Area Network)*
A network that connects computers over long distances via telephone lines or satellite links. In a wide area network, the computers are physically and sometimes geographically far apart.

Web Editor
A person in charge of maintaining the visual and editorial elements of, as well as the navigation of, a web site.

Web Master
A person in charge of technically maintaining a web site.

Web Page
A document created with HTML (HyperText Markup Language) that is part of a group of hypertext documents or resources available on the World Wide Web. Collectively, these documents and resources form what is known as a web site.

Web Site
The collection of network services, primarily HTML documents, that is linked together and exists on the Web at a particular server. Exploring a web site usually begins with the home page, which may lead you to more information about that site. A single server may support multiple web sites.

WinSock *(Windows Sockets)*
Describes the Microsoft Windows implementation of TCP/IP. You use it if you directly connect your Windows PC to the Internet, either with a permanent connection or with a modem.

WinZip
A compression program for Windows that allows you to zip and unzip ZIP files as well as other standard types of archive files.

World Wide Web
The graphical extension to the Internet.

X.12
An international standard for electronic data interchange. New e-commerce standards like OBI are based on older established standards like X.12.

Index